500 RECIPES FOR MEALS IN MINUTES

by Catherine Kirkpatrick

HAMLYN

Contents

Cover photograph by Paul Williams

Published by Hamlyn Publishing
Astronaut House, Feltham, Middlesex, England

© Copyright Hamlyn Publishing 1964
a division of The Hamlyn Publishing Group Limited

First published 1964
Revised edition 1971
Sixteenth impression 1985

ISBN 0 600 36019 9

Printed and bound in Great Britain by
R. J. Acford

Introduction

Have you ever stopped to think of the number of meals that you serve in a year, the amount of time spent in planning, shopping, preparing and cooking? You would probably be astounded if you had the time to work out the answer! If you are like most of us doing a 9–5 job, you are probably very familiar with that feeling of desperation that comes when all meals have to be prepared with one eye on the clock. If you do share that feeling then this is the book for you. It is not a book to browse through, not a book of 'gimmicky' recipes. This is a collection of practical every-day recipes, almost all of which can be cooked in 30 minutes or under. You will not find that there are many convenience foods used in this book. Most manufacturers supply their own recipes for using their products, and in many cases you do not really need recipes at all. But do not be afraid to take short cuts with your cooking. The shelves of the grocer's shop and the supermarkets are stacked with ingredients for real gourmet cooking and dishes which, at one time would have taken hours to prepare, can now be completed in a matter of minutes and no one but you need know that many of the ingredients started off in a packet or a can. Anyway, why be ashamed of using convenience foods. Food manufacturers today draw on the experience and knowledge of food technologists from all over the world and prepare products all aimed at making the job of the housewife easier, at the same time ensuring that she will get the best results from all her cooking. Packet sauces for example – all the tiresome work has been done for you, simply add milk and cook for a few minutes and there is no longer any need to worry about the sauce lumping. Frozen vegetables, pastry, chicken joints, boil in the bag rice, canned puddings, there is a tremendous variety of convenient foods to choose from. If you are jealous of your reputation as a cook, you can add your own touches and still feel satisfied that you are giving your family appetizing and nourishing meals.

You will not find many recipes for puddings and desserts included. If you are really trying to beat the clock you will find that fruit or cheese is the ideal way of finishing the meal, and diet conscious adults are usually happy to skip the sweet course. And for the children – fruit and custard, ice cream, jelly – these old-fashioned sweets are still very acceptable in this modern space-age world. However, you will find a selection of recipes for puddings and home-made cakes and biscuits for the occasion when you would be happier to say 'Yes, I made it myself.'

If you are faced with the problem of serving meals in a hurry for unexpected guests, it is worth having some pet recipes up your sleeve and a few special ingredients in the store cupboard. Packet soups do not take up much space and can be used as an appetizing first course, served with cheese and biscuits to make a quick meal, and they can also be used to give flavour to a variety of stew and casserole type dishes. Canned celery and sweet corn are also useful for a special meal in an emergency. A can of prepared mix for making ice cream at home, canned fruit and evaporated milk and packet jelly are all good stand-bys.

Here is a quick and tasty meal that can be prepared in half an hour and one that you would be proud to serve on any occasion. Chicken joints fried in oil until golden, served with a colourful salad made by tossing together a can of sweet corn niblets, with a medley of cooked frozen vegetables, chopped eating apple and currants. To follow there is a choice of ice cream (prepared mix), or fruit flan. Who would guess that this was a bought flan case filled with drained canned fruit and jelly? There is coffee to finish, of course.

Some Useful Facts and Figures

Notes on metrication

In case you wish to convert quantities into metric measures, the following tables give a comparison.

Solid measures

Ounces	Approx. grams to nearest whole figure	Recommended conversion to nearest unit of 25
1	28	25
2	57	50
3	85	75
4	113	100
5	142	150
6	170	175
7	198	200
8	227	225
9	255	250
10	283	275
11	312	300
12	340	350
13	368	375
14	396	400
15	425	425
16 (1 lb)	454	450
17	482	475
18	510	500
19	539	550
20 ($1\frac{1}{4}$ lb)	567	575

Note: When converting quantities over 20 oz first add the appropriate figures in the centre column, then adjust to the nearest unit of 25. As a general guide, 1 kg (1000 g) equals 2·2 lb or about 2 lb 3 oz. This method of conversion gives good results in nearly all cases, although in certain pastry and cake recipes a more accurate conversion is necessary to produce a balanced recipe.

Liquid measures

Imperial	Approx. millilitres to nearest whole figure	Recommended millilitres
$\frac{1}{4}$ pint	142	150
$\frac{1}{2}$ pint	283	300
$\frac{3}{4}$ pint	425	450
1 pint	567	600
$1\frac{1}{2}$ pints	851	900
$1\frac{3}{4}$ pints	992	1000 (1 litre)

Oven temperatures

The table below gives recommended equivalents.

	°C	°F	Gas Mark
Very cool	110	225	$\frac{1}{4}$
	120	250	$\frac{1}{2}$
Cool	140	275	1
	150	300	2
Moderate	160	325	3
	180	350	4
Moderately hot	190	375	5
	200	400	6
Hot	220	425	7
	230	450	8
Very hot	240	475	9

Notes for American and Australian users

In America the 8-oz measuring cup is used. In Australia metric measures are now used in conjunction with the standard 250-ml measuring cup. The Imperial pint, used in Britain and Australia, is 20 fl oz, while the American pint is 16 fl. oz. It is important to remember that the Australian tablespoon differs from both the British and American tablespoons; the table below gives a comparison. The British standard tablespoon, which has been used throughout this book, holds 17·7 ml, the American 14·2 ml, and the Australian 20 ml. A teaspoon holds approximately 5 ml in all three countries.

Hors-d'oeuvre

No part of a meal lends itself so much to the imagination as the appetizer or hors-d'oeuvre. It is meant to whet the appetite for the food which is to follow and so must look tempting, and be served in small quantities.

The choice of an hors-d'oeuvre must depend very much on the dishes which are to follow but for meals in a hurry something simple must be chosen. There is a wide choice of fruits, eggs, vegetables, fish or meat and when time is limited make use of the canned and prepared foods on the market. A mixture of fruit and sea food makes a very popular hors-d'oeuvre.

Grapefruit hors-d'oeuvre

To prepare grapefruit

Allow half for each person, use a sharp pointed knife and cut round between the skin and the fruit, then loosen each section and remove the core.

With sugar: Sprinkle lightly with sugar and serve as cold as possible. Put a maraschino cherry or a mint leaf in the centre before serving.

Grapefruit and orange cocktail

Use canned grapefruit, or remove the segments from fresh grapefruit and arrange in small dishes alternately with segments of mandarin oranges. Garnish with a sprig of mint.

Grapefruit and ginger cocktail

Arrange segments of fresh or canned grapefruit in small glasses, add 2 teaspoons ginger syrup and 1 tablespoon finely chopped preserved ginger.

Grapefruit and crab cocktail

Remove the segments from 2 grapefruits. Add the contents of 1 4-oz. can crab. Bind with a little mayonnaise and serve in the grapefruit shells. Garnish with lemon or a sprig of water-cress.

Hot grapefruit

Halve and prepare fresh grapefruit in the ordinary way. Sprinkle with brown sugar and add a knob of butter. Put under a hot grill until the top is nicely browned. For special occasions, 1 teaspoon brandy, rum or sherry can be added before grilling.

Melon hors-d'oeuvre

To prepare melon

Honeydew and cantaloupe melon should be served as cold as possible. Cut into slices and serve with sugar and powdered ginger, or with lemon. Charentais melon, which is usually more expensive, should be cut through the centre and served with sugar.

Melon and shrimp cocktail

Cut the melon into dice or scoop out balls with a vegetable ball cutter. Add the contents of 1 4-oz. can shrimps. Arrange in small cocktail glasses. Cover with 1 tablespoon mayonnaise to which a little tomato purée has been added. Garnish with shrimps.

Avocado hors-d'oeuvre

To prepare avocado

Allow 1 pear for 2 persons.
Wipe but do not peel, cut the pear in half lengthwise with a stainless knife and remove the stone.
Serve with French dressing (see page 82).

Avocado pear with shrimps

Prepare the pear as above, then fill the cavity with shrimps moistened with a little French dressing (see page 82).

Avocado and grapefruit

Peel and slice the pears and leave for about

10 minutes covered with French dressing (see page 82). Arrange on plates with alternate sections of grapefruit. Garnish with a thin slice of cucumber.

Fish cocktails and hors-d'oeuvre

Basic cocktail sauce

you will need:

3 tablespoons mayonnaise	2 tablespoons thin cream
1 tablespoon Worcester sauce	salt and pepper little lemon juice

Mix all the ingredients together.

Tomato cocktail sauce: Add 1 tablespoon tomato purée to the basic sauce above.

Shrimp cocktail

you will need:

small quantity lettuce	3 tablespoons plain or
1 4–oz. can shrimps	tomato cocktail sauce
	little paprika

1 Shred the lettuce and put a little into the bottom of small glasses.
2 Arrange the shrimps on top.
3 Cover with cocktail sauce.
4 Sprinkle with paprika and garnish with lemon. Serve as cold as possible.

With other shellfish: Lobster or crab can be used in place of shrimps.

Tuna cocktail

you will need:

1 small can tuna fillets	3 tablespoons plain or
watercress	tomato cocktail sauce
	1 dessertspoon vinegar

1 Drain the oil from the fish and break the fish up into small pieces.
2 Chop the watercress and mix with the fish.
3 Add the cocktail sauce and the vinegar.
4 Put into small glasses and garnish with a sprig of watercress.

Smoked salmon

Except for special occasions this may be considered too expensive, but the prepared frozen smoked salmon now available makes a very popular hors-d'oeuvre.

To serve: Be sure the salmon is cut into very thin slices and that it is moist and oily. Generally allow 3–4 oz. for 3 people. Serve cayenne or paprika pepper and garnish with wedges of lemon. Serve with thin rolled brown bread and butter.

To make the rolled bread: Cut the crusts from slices of thinly cut, buttered brown bread and roll up.

Salmon and asparagus rolls

Wrap a thin slice of smoked salmon round a spear of canned or fresh cooked asparagus. Serve as above with brown bread and butter, wedges of lemon and cayenne pepper.

Smoked trout

These can be bought already smoked, and require very little preparation. Remove the skin, make an incision down the centre and remove the fillet, then turn over and do the same. Serve with horseradish cream, wedges of lemon and rolled brown bread and butter as above.

Vegetable hors-d'oeuvre

Tomato juice cocktail 1

you will need:

1 can tomato juice	1 tablespoon lemon juice
1 teaspoon Worcester sauce	salt and pepper
pinch sugar	mint leaves

1 Mix all the ingredients well together and season carefully with salt and pepper, preferably freshly ground black pepper.
2 Chill thoroughly, then serve in glasses garnished with a leaf or small sprig of mint.

If you have a little more time to spare the following makes an excellent cocktail.

Tomato juice cocktail 2

you will need:

½ pint tomato juice
1 tablespoon lemon juice
1 dessertspoon freshly grated horseradish
2 teaspoons parsley, chopped
1 stick celery, chopped
1 small onion, finely chopped
salt
whipped cream

1 Mix all the ingredients and chill thoroughly.
2 Strain and serve in tall glasses with 1 teaspoon whipped cream on top.

Fresh mushroom hors-d'oeuvre

you will need:

8 oz. button mushrooms
juice 1 lemon
3 tablespoons oil
salt
freshly ground black pepper
1 level teaspoon chives, finely chopped
2 level teaspoons parsley, finely chopped

1 Rinse and dry the mushrooms, but do not peel.
2 Slice very thinly.
3 Make a dressing with the lemon juice, oil and seasoning and pour over the mushrooms.
4 Leave as long as possible before serving.
5 Sprinkle with the chives and parsley.

Artichokes

you will need:

1 artichoke per person
melted butter or hollandaise sauce (see page 82)

1 Wash and remove the stem.
2 Remove any discoloured or coarse leaves from the outside.
3 Remove the choke (i.e. the feathery part) from the centre.
4 Cook in boiling salted water until tender, about 20 minutes.
5 Strain off the water and place the artichokes upside-down to drain.
6 Serve cold with melted butter or hollandaise sauce.

Stuffed tomatoes

These make a colourful and attractive hors-d'oeuvre, and an endless variety of fillings can be prepared quickly.

To prepare the tomato case:
1 Choose firm and even-sized tomatoes and cut a slice from the stem end.
2 Remove the pulp with a small teaspoon, being careful not to split the tomato. Leave upside-down to drain.

Suggestions for fillings

Egg and caper: Mix the tomato pulp with scrambled egg and a few chopped capers. Season carefully and pile into the tomato cases. Garnish with a sprig of parsley.

Chicken or ham: Mix the tomato pulp with finely chopped chicken or ham mixed with a little mayonnaise. Season carefully and add a few shredded almonds.

Cheese and pineapple: Mix the tomato pulp with grated cheese and finely chopped pineapple. Season carefully.

Sweet corn niblets: Mix the sweet corn with the tomato pulp. Season carefully and pile into the tomato cases.

Quick Soups

Soup is always popular, whether it is served as the start of a full-course meal, or to provide more nourishment with a light snack. And there is no reason to feel that you cannot attempt soup making because you have no time to prepare the stock. In all of the recipes in the following chapter, a cube of chicken or meat stock may be used, if home-made stock is not available. However, if cubes are used, you must remember that extra seasoning may not be necessary.

Consommé

cooking time: about 10 minutes

you will need for 4 servings:

1½ pints chicken stock	salt and pepper
2 tablespoons sherry	croûtons or parsley to
squeeze lemon juice	garnish

1 Heat the chicken stock.
2 Add sherry and lemon juice.
3 Add seasoning as required.
4 Serve with croûtons or sprinkle with parsley.

To make croûtons

1 Cut some day old bread into small dice or fancy shapes and fry in hot fat. Drain well before using.
2 Make some toast and cut into dice.

Consommé à la princesse

cooking time: about 10 minutes

you will need for 4 servings:

4 oz. cooked chicken	4 oz. cooked green
1½ pints chicken stock	peas
	salt and pepper

1 Shred the chicken.
2 Put into a pan with the chicken stock and peas and heat well.
3 Add seasoning as required.

Jellied consommé

cooking time: about 15 minutes

you will need for 4 servings:

2 pints chicken stock	1 tablespoon lemon
½ oz. gelatine	juice
2 tablespoons sherry	1 egg white
	1 egg shell, crushed

1 Put all the ingredients together in a large pan.
2 Heat to boiling point, whisking all the time.
3 Simmer for 5 minutes, then strain through a piece of double muslin.
4 Season as necessary and leave to set.
5 Break up with a fork and serve well chilled.

Tomato consommé: Follow the recipe as above and add 1 small can tomato purée to the other ingredients.

Hollandaise soup

cooking time: 15–20 minutes

you will need for 4 servings:

1 oz. butter	salt
½ oz. cornflour	grated nutmeg
1 pint chicken stock	3 tablespoons cooked
2 egg yolks	green peas
¼ pint thin cream	

1 Melt the butter in a pan.
2 Add the cornflour and cook for a few minutes.
3 Add the stock, stir until boiling and simmer for 5 minutes.
4 Leave to cool a little.
5 Mix the egg yolks and cream together and strain carefully into the cooked soup.
6 Reheat without boiling.
7 Add salt to taste and a pinch of nutmeg.
8 Put the peas into a hot tureen and pour the soup over.

Chicken and celery soup

cooking time: about 20 minutes

you will need for 4 servings:

4 oz. celery	1 egg
1½ pints chicken stock	½ pint milk
4 oz. cooked chicken	salt and pepper
1 oz. flour	grated cheese

1 Chop the celery into small pieces. Cook in the chicken stock until tender.
2 Dice the chicken and add to the stock.
3 Mix the flour, egg and milk together smoothly and stir into the other ingredients.
4 Heat carefully until the soup thickens.
5 Correct the seasoning and serve with grated cheese.

Watercress soup

cooking time: about 30 minutes

you will need for 4 servings:

2 bundles watercress	¼ pint milk
1 oz. butter	3 tablespoons thin
1 pint chicken stock	cream
½ oz. flour	salt and pepper

1 Wash the watercress and chop coarsely.
2 Melt the butter and sauté the watercress for a few minutes.
3 Add stock, simmer for about 15 minutes.
4 Rub through a sieve and return to the pan.
5 Mix the flour smoothly with the milk, add to the purée and stir until boiling.

6 Simmer for 3 minutes. Correct the seasoning.
7 Just before serving, add the cream and, if liked, a few drops of green food colouring.
8 Garnish with sprigs of watercress.

Carrot soup

cooking time: about 25–30 minutes

you will need for 4 servings:

1 lb. carrots	salt and pepper
1 onion or leek	*bouquet garni*
½ small turnip	½ pint milk
1 oz. butter	1 tablespoon finely
1 pint stock or water	chopped parsley

1 Prepare the vegetables and grate them finely.
2 Heat the butter in a pan, add the vegetables and sauté all well together.
3 Add the stock, salt and pepper and the *bouquet garni.*
4 Cover and simmer until the vegetables are tender.
5 Remove the *bouquet garni.*
6 Add the milk, reheat the soup and correct the seasoning.
7 Just before serving, add the parsley.

Cheese soup

cooking time: about 25 minutes

you will need for 4 servings

2 medium-sized potatoes	4 oz. Cheddar cheese
1 onion	3–4 tablespoons thin cream
1 carrot	salt and pepper
1 stick celery	little chopped parsley
1 pint stock or water	

1 Prepare and dice the vegetables.
2 Put into a pan with the stock and simmer until tender, about 15 minutes.
3 Stir in the grated cheese and cream.
4 Add seasonings as required and add parsley just before serving.

Vegetable soup

cooking time: about 30 minutes

you will need for 4 servings:

2 onions	3 oz. cooked green peas or 1 small packet frozen peas
8 oz. potatoes	
8 oz. turnips	
2 oz. butter	1 level tablespoon cornflour
1 pint water	
salt and pepper	½ pint milk

1 Slice the onions thinly and cut the other vegetables into thin strips.
2 Sauté all in the butter for a few minutes.
3 Add the water, bring to the boil, cover and simmer for about 15 minutes, until the vegetables are tender.
4 Add seasoning as required and add the peas.
5 Mix the cornflour smoothly with the milk, stir into the soup. Stir until boiling and cook for 2 minutes longer.

Clam soup

cooking time: 15–20 minutes

you will need for 4 servings:

1 oz. butter	1 7½-oz. can minced clams
little grated onion	
½ oz. flour	salt and pepper
½ pint white stock	pinch celery salt
½ pint milk	little chopped parsley
	grated cheese

1 Melt the butter and sauté the onion for a few minutes.
2 Add the flour and mix well, cook for a few minutes longer.
3 Add the stock and milk gradually. Stir until boiling and boil for 1 minute.
4 Add the clams and reheat without boiling.
5 Add salt and pepper as required and the celery salt.
6 Sprinkle with parsley before serving and serve grated cheese separately.

Summer soup

cooking time: about 25 minutes

you will need for 4 servings:

2 pints stock or water	½ small lettuce
2 oz. sago	1 sprig mint
3–4 carrots	8 oz. shelled green peas
2–3 oz. runner beans	
1 small onion	salt and pepper

1 Heat the stock to boiling point, add the sago.
2 Dice the carrots and beans, chop the onion finely.
3 Shred the lettuce and chop the mint.
4 Add all the ingredients to the pan with a little salt and pepper.
5 Cover and simmer until the vegetables are tender and the sago is cooked.

Autumn chowder

cooking time: 30 minutes

you will need for 4 servings:

2 tablespoons corn oil	2 sticks celery, diced
1 onion, finely chopped	12-oz. can sweetcorn
1 packet tomato soup	kernels
1 pint water	8 oz. cooked cod,
½ pint milk	flaked
1 large potato, diced	3 slices bread, toasted

1 Heat the corn oil and sauté the onion for a few minutes.
2 Add the contents of the packet of tomato soup and stir in the water and milk. Bring to the boil, stirring occasionally.
3 Stir in the potato and celery and simmer gently for 15 minutes.
4 Add the corn, well drained, and the fish. Cook for a further 10 minutes.
5 Cut the toast into small triangles and place on top of each individual serving.

Liver soup

cooking time: about 30 minutes

you will need for 4 servings:

8 oz. liver	2 pints brown stock or
2 level tablespoons	stock made with
flour	beef cubes
4 oz. mushrooms	1 carrot
1 oz. dripping	1 onion

1 Cut the liver into very small pieces and coat with flour.
2 Chop the mushrooms and put with the liver.
3 Heat the dripping in a pan, add the liver and mushrooms and any remaining flour and sauté all for a few minutes.
4 Add the stock and the carrot, chopped finely, and stir until boiling.
4 Cover and simmer about 25 minutes or until the liver is quite tender.
6 Correct the seasoning.
7 Garnish with the onion cut into thin rings and sautéed in a little butter.

Potato and leek soup

cooking time: about 25 minutes

you will need for 4 servings:

1 rasher of bacon	2–3 tablespoons thin
1 oz. butter	cream or top of the
1 lb. potatoes	milk
3 leeks	parsley
1 pint stock or water	grated cheese
salt and pepper	

1 Chop the bacon and fry lightly in a saucepan.
2 Add the butter.
3 Chop the potatoes and leeks and sauté in the fat for a few minutes.
4 Add the stock and salt and pepper.
5 Cover and simmer for about 20 minutes.
6 Add the cream.
7 Just before serving add chopped parsley and serve with grated cheese.

Onion soup

cooking time: about 30 minutes

you will need for 4 servings:

1 lb. onions	½ pint milk
1 oz. butter	3–4 tablespoons
¾ pint stock	croûtons (see page
bouquet garni	8)
2 level tablespoons	grated cheese
flour	

1 Slice the onions thinly and cook slowly in the butter until tender.
2 Add the stock and *bouquet garni*.
3 Cover and simmer for about 20 minutes.
4 Mix the flour smoothly with the milk and stir into the soup.
5 Stir until boiling and boil for 1 minute.
6 Season as required.
7 Put the croûtons into a soup tureen and pour the soup over.
8 Sprinkle with cheese or serve it separately.

Vegetable marrow soup

cooking time: about 25 minutes

you will need for 4 servings:

2–2½ lb. marrow	*bouquet garni*
1 oz. butter	½ oz. cornflour
1 pint stock or water	½ pint milk
salt and pepper	grated cheese

1 Peel and seed the marrow and cut into small pieces.
2 Melt the butter in a pan, add the marrow and sauté for a few minutes.
3 Add the stock, seasonings and *bouquet garni*.
4 Cover and simmer until the marrow is quite soft.
5 Remove the *bouquet garni* and mash the marrow with a wooden spoon or vegetable masher.
6 Mix the cornflour smoothly with the milk. Add

to the soup, stir until boiling and boil for 1 minute.

7 Correct the seasoning, add a few drops of green food colouring, if liked, and serve with grated cheese.

Chicken cream soup

cooking time: about 25 minutes

you will need for 4 servings:

1 oz. butter	1 egg yolk
1 oz. cornflour or	celery salt
arrowroot	chopped parsley
2 pints chicken stock	croûtons (see page 8)
1 bay leaf	

1 Melt the butter, add the cornflour and mix well.
2 Add the stock, stir until boiling.
3 Add the bay leaf and simmer 15 minutes.
4 Remove the bay leaf and allow the soup to cool a little.
5 Mix the egg yolk with a little of the soup, add to the rest of the soup and reheat without boiling.
6 Add celery salt and seasoning to taste.
7 Just before serving add a little chopped parsley and serve with croûtons.

Cold soups

Lemon bongo soup

cooking time: 10–15 minutes

you will need for 4 servings:

2 egg yolks	¼ pint thin cream
½ oz. cornflour	2 oz. cooked Patna rice
1½ pints chicken stock	½ oz. toasted shredded
juice ¼ lemon	almonds

1 Mix the egg yolks and cornflour with a little of the cold stock or water.
2 Add to the rest of the stock, heat gently to boiling point, then simmer for 3 minutes, stirring all the time.
3 Cool, then add lemon juice, cream and cooked rice.

Fish Dishes

4 Chill thoroughly and serve sprinkled with shredded almonds.

Vichyssoise soup

cooking time: about 30 minutes

you will need for 4 servings:

8 oz. potatoes	1½ pints white stock
1 leek	(or chicken stock
6 spring onions	cube)
8 oz. green peas	½ pint milk
sprig of fresh mint	½ oz. cornflour
salt and pepper	½ oz. butter
	¼ pint thin cream

1 Prepare and chop the potatoes, leek and spring onions, and put into a pan with the peas, mint and stock.
2 Simmer until tender, then rub through a sieve.
3 Mix the cornflour smoothly with a little of the milk.
4 Put the rest of the milk on to heat with the butter.
5 Add to the mixed cornflour and stir until boiling.
6 Add this sauce to the purée and mix well.
7 Correct the seasoning and add the cream.
8 Chill thoroughly.

Cucumber soup

cooking time: about 25 minutes

you will need for 4 servings:

1 large cucumber	little cold milk or water
6 spring onions	salt and pepper
1½ pints chicken stock	¼ pint thin cream
1 oz. flour	few drops green food
	colouring

1 Peel and chop cucumber, chop onions, and simmer in the stock until the cucumber is tender.
2 Rub through a sieve then return to the pan.
3 Mix the flour smoothly with a little cold milk or water, add to the soup, stir until boiling and simmer for 3 minutes.
4 Season as required and add the cream.
5 Add a few drops of green colouring and chill thoroughly.

When you want to prepare a meal in a hurry, fish is always an excellent choice. It is an ex-tremely nutritious food, the cooking time is usually short, and if prepared with a little care and imagination, it makes a delicious main dish. I hope you will find that the recipes in the following chapter will provide you with a number of interesting new ideas.

General methods of cooking fish

To fry fish

Small whole fish, such as herrings, mackerel, haddock, plaice, sole, whiting or steaks of cod, halibut, hake, should be used.

1 Herrings and mackerel are generally fried in shallow fat or oil. Other fish can be fried in shallow or deep fat.
2 Clean and prepare the fish according to its kind.
3 Coat with flour to which salt and pepper has been added.
4 Or coat with egg and breadcrumbs or with batter.
5 Fry until golden brown, then reduce the heat and fry until the flakes begin to separate.
6 Drain well on kitchen paper.
7 Serve with maître d'hôtel butter (see page 13).

To grill fish

Use fish as for frying.
1 Heat the grill and brush the grill rack with a little melted butter or oil.
2 Season the fish, brush with oil or melted butter.
3 Grill for 2 minutes on both sides, then reduce the heat and continue the cooking until the fish is cooked.

To bake fish

Whole fish, as above, or steaks or fillets of fish are suitable.
This is a popular method as no flavour is lost in the cooking. Baked fish is often stuffed before cooking.
1 Prepare the fish according to its kind and stuff if required.
2 Put into a baking dish with a little hot butter or dripping.

3 Baste with the hot fat and if liked sprinkle with a few breadcrumbs.
4 Bake in a moderately hot oven (375°F – Gas Mark 5), allowing approximately 10 minutes to each 1 lb. of fish plus 5 minutes over, e.g. a piece of fish weighing 2 lb. would take approximately 25 minutes to cook.
5 Serve on a hot dish garnished with lemon and parsley and with a suitable sauce.

To boil fish

This method is suitable for large fish which have a good natural flavour, e.g. salmon or turbot.
To improve the flavour of boiled fish, seasoning and flavouring should be added to the water in which the fish is cooked, or chicken stock may be used.

you will need:

2 pints water	bouquet garni
1 tablespoon vinegar	1 carrot
4–6 peppercorns	1 onion
1 onion stuck with 2 cloves	salt

1 Combine above ingredients, bring to boil.
2 Tie the fish loosely in a piece of muslin, put into the boiling water, cover and simmer very gently. For thick fish allow 10 minutes to each 1 lb. and 10 minutes over, e.g. a 2 lb. fish should simmer 30 minutes.
3 Remove the fish carefully, drain well and serve with a good sauce. (For sauce recipes to serve with fish, see page 21.)

Batters for coating fish

Batter 1

you will need:

2 oz. flour	1 level teaspoon baking powder (if plain flour is used)
¼ teaspoon salt	
pinch pepper	
4 tablespoons milk	

1 Sift all dry ingredients together and mix to a smooth paste with a little of the cold milk.
2 Add the rest of the milk and beat well. Use at once.

Batter 2

you will need:

2 oz. flour	1 dessertspoon oil
pinch salt	1 egg white
4 dessertspoons tepid water	

1 Mix flour and salt together.
2 Add water and oil and mix all smoothly.
3 Beat the egg white stiffly and fold into the batter.

Maître d'hôtel butter

(to serve with fish)

you will need:

1 oz. butter	little cayenne pepper
2 tablespoons finely chopped parsley	few drops lemon juice

1 Beat the butter till creamy.
2 Add all other ingredients.
3 Form into a neat pat and leave in a cool place till required.

Fish meunière

cooking time: about 10–15 minutes

you will need for 4 servings:

1 lb. white fish (sole, plaice or any white fish can be used)	about 4 oz. butter, for frying
1 tablespoon flour	4 teaspoons lemon juice
salt and pepper	

1 Prepare the fish and coat with flour to which salt and pepper has been added.
2 Heat most of the butter in a shallow pan and fry the fish on both sides until golden brown and well cooked.
3 Put on to a serving dish and keep hot.
4 Add the remaining butter to the pan and heat until it begins to brown.
5 Add the lemon juice and pour over the fish.
6 Garnish with lemon and parsley.

Fish portugaise

cooking time: 20–25 minutes

you will need for 4 servings:

1 lb. fillets white fish	2 tablespoons grated cheese
salt and pepper	2 tablespoons breadcrumbs
lemon juice	
1 small onion, sliced very thinly	½ oz. butter
4 tomatoes, peeled and sliced	

1 Trim the fish, season with salt and pepper and lemon juice and arrange in a fireproof dish.
2 Add the onion and tomatoes.
3 Mix the cheese and breadcrumbs together and sprinkle on top.
4 Dot with butter and bake about 20 minutes in a moderate oven (350°F – Gas Mark 4).

Fish maître d'hôtel

cooking time: 15–20 minutes

you will need for 4 servings:

1 lb. fillets white fish (sole, plaice or haddock)	lemon juice
salt and pepper	¼ pint maître d'hôtel sauce (see page 22)

1 Prepare the fish and season each fillet with salt and pepper and a squeeze of lemon juice.
2 Fold each fillet in half with the skinned side inside. Arrange in a lightly greased fireproof dish.
3 Cover and cook in a moderate oven (350°F – Gas Mark 4) for 10–15 minutes.
4 Remove the fillets to a serving dish and coat with the maître d'hôtel sauce.
5 Garnish with lemon and parsley.

Fish bonne femme

cooking time: 20 minutes – depending on thickness of fillets

you will need for 4 servings:

4 fillets of sole (plaice or any white fish may be used)	1 teaspoon parsley, chopped
	salt and pepper
4 oz. mushrooms, thinly sliced	¼ pint white wine or cider
1 shallot or small piece of onion, chopped	¼ pint white sauce (see page 21)
	½ oz. butter

1 Put the fish into a pan with the mushrooms, onion, parsley and seasoning.
2 Cover with the wine and poach very gently until cooked.
3 Remove the fish carefully on to a serving dish.
4 Continue to boil the remaining liquid until it is reduced by half.
5 Add to the hot sauce and stir in the butter.
6 Pour over the fish and brown under the grill.

13

Casserole of fish

cooking time: 25–30 minutes

you will need for 4 servings:

1½ lb. fillets of fresh haddock	pinch paprika
	pinch nutmeg
1 oz. butter	milk
1 medium-sized onion, thinly sliced	2 eggs
	1 oz. flour
salt and pepper	juice 1 lemon

1 Prepare the fish and cut into pieces and put into a casserole.
2 Melt the butter and cook the onion until soft.
3 Sprinkle the onion on top of the fish and add salt, pepper, paprika and nutmeg.
4 Moisten with a little milk and water. Cover and bake for about 15 minutes in a moderately hot oven (375°F – Gas Mark 5).
5 Mix the eggs, flour and lemon juice together. Add any liquid from the fish and mix in well.
6 Pour over the fish, return to the oven and cook uncovered for a further 10 minutes.

Baked stuffed haddock

cooking time: 20–25 minutes

you will need for 4 servings:

1 fresh haddock

For stuffing:

1 oz. breadcrumbs	salt and pepper
1 oz. butter	pinch mixed herbs
1 teaspoon finely chopped parsley	egg or milk to bind
	a little flour
½ teaspoon grated lemon rind	egg and breadcrumbs
	1 oz. butter

1 Wash and trim the fish but do not remove the head.
2 Make a stuffing by mixing all the ingredients together except for the flour, egg and crumbs and 1 oz. butter.
3 Place the stuffing in the fish and secure with thread or a skewer.
4 Rub the fish over with flour, then coat with egg and breadcrumbs.
5 Heat the butter in a baking tin, put in the fish, baste with the hot butter and bake in a moderate oven (350°F – Gas Mark 4), basting frequently.
6 Garnish with lemon and parsley and serve with anchovy sauce (see page 21).

Note

If liked, the fish may be trussed into an 'S' shape or a circle. To do this, the fish must be sewn up securely and not held with a skewer.

Cod steaks Valencia

cooking time: 15–20 minutes

you will need for 4 servings:

4 cod steaks	1 oz. butter
2 tablespoons white wine	grated rind ½ orange
	salt and pepper
3 tablespoons orange juice	

1 Prepare the fish and put it into a fireproof dish.
2 Pour over the wine and orange juice and leave for 10 minutes.
3 Mix the butter with the grated orange rind and put in small pieces over the fish. Season with salt and pepper.
4 Cover the dish tightly with a lid, or cover with aluminium foil and bake in a moderate oven (350°F – Gas Mark 4) for about 20 minutes.
5 Drain off the liquor from the fish, put into a small pan and reduce a little by boiling and then pour over the fish.
6 Garnish with segments of orange.

Devonshire cod

cooking time: 20–25 minutes

you will need for 4 servings:

1 lb. cod fillet	½ pint cider
salt and pepper	1 oz. butter
1–2 tomatoes, peeled and sliced	1 oz. cornflour
	8 oz. mashed potato
2 oz. mushrooms, sliced	grated cheese

1 Cut the fish into pieces and put into a fireproof dish.
2 Season and add tomatoes and mushrooms.
3 Pour on the cider and bake about 15 minutes in a moderately hot oven (375°F – Gas Mark 5).
4 Strain off the liquor, add the butter and thicken with the cornflour.
5 Correct the seasoning and pour the sauce over the fish.
6 Pipe the potato round the edge of the dish, sprinkle with cheese and return to the oven to brown.

Mushroom cod

cooking time: 35 minutes

you will need for 4 servings:

1 lb. cod fillet	1 packet mushroom
1 oz. cornflour	sauce
salt and pepper	milk
1 tablespoon corn oil	*To garnish:*
1 small onion, finely	chopped parsley
chopped	
4 oz. mushrooms,	
thinly sliced	

1 Skin the cod and cut into three portions. Wash and dry well.
2 Coat with the cornflour to which salt and pepper have been added.
3 Put a piece of foil on to a baking sheet. Place the cod on top.
4 Heat the corn oil. Add the onion and mushrooms and fry until soft. Spoon over the cod.
5 Fold over the sides of the foil and bring both ends up to overlap forming a parcel.
6 Cook in a moderately hot oven (375°F – Gas Mark 5) for 30 minutes. Open the foil and drain the liquor into a measuring jug.
7 Arrange the cod on a warmed serving dish.
8 Make up the sauce as directed on the packet, using the fish liquor made up to ½ pint with milk.
9 Pour the sauce over the cod and sprinkle with chopped parsley.

Devilled fish

cooking time: 20–25 minutes

you will need for 4 servings:

1½–2 lb. fillets of	2 shallots, finely
white fish	chopped
¼ pint dry white wine	1 teaspoon dry
4 tablespoons water	mustard
1 tablespoon oil	½ level teaspoon curry
1 tablespoon finely	powder
chopped parsley	salt and pepper

1 Put the fish into a greased fireproof dish.
2 Mix the wine, water, oil, parsley and shallots.
3 Mix the mustard and curry powder smoothly with a little warm water and add to the rest of the liquid.
4 Add a little seasoning and pour over the fish.
5 Bake in a moderate oven (350°F – Gas Mark 4) until the fish is cooked and flakes easily.

Fish and bacon rolls

cooking time: about 20 minutes

you will need for 4 servings:

4 good-sized fillets	lemon juice
plaice or sole	salt and pepper
4 rashers bacon	toast

1 Trim the fillets.
2 Remove the rind from the bacon rashers and place a fillet on each rasher.
3 Sprinkle with lemon juice and a little salt and pepper and roll up. If necessary, secure with a wooden cocktail stick.
4 Bake in a moderately hot oven (375°F – Gas Mark 5).
5 Serve on hot buttered toast.

Fresh haddock with cider

cooking time: 20–25 minutes

you will need for 4 servings:

1½–2 lb. fresh haddock	½ lemon, cut into thick
fillet	slices
2 oz. butter	salt and pepper
¼ pint cider	little chopped parsley
2–3 tomatoes, peeled	1 small shallot,
and sliced	chopped finely
4–6 mushrooms,	
sliced	

1 Cut the fish into pieces and put into a greased fireproof dish.
2 Put small pieces of butter on top and then add the cider.
3 Cover with tomatoes, mushrooms and lemon.
4 Season carefully, cover and bake in a moderately hot oven (375°F – Gas Mark 5).
5 Before serving, sprinkle with parsley and shallot.

Scalloped haddock

cooking time: 25–30 minutes

you will need for 4 servings:

1 lb. smoked haddock	1 pint cheese sauce
8 oz. spaghetti	(see page 22)
2 rashers streaky	breadcrumbs
bacon, diced	little grated nutmeg
2 onions, finely	little butter
chopped	

1 Cook the haddock, remove the skin and bone and flake finely.

2 Cook the spaghetti in boiling, salted water.

3 Fry the bacon, add the onions and cook in the bacon fat until soft.

4 Mix the fish, spaghetti, bacon and onion together in a casserole and pour over the cheese sauce.

5 Sprinkle with breadcrumbs and nutmeg, dot with butter and bake in a moderate oven (350°F – Gas Mark 4).

Halibut with mimosa sauce

cooking time: about 20 minutes

you will need for 4 servings:

2 steaks halibut (allowing 1 steak for 2 persons)	salt, pepper and lemon juice
	½ oz. butter
	little milk

To make sauce:

¾ oz. butter	2 hard-boiled eggs
¾ oz. flour	salt and pepper
¼ pint milk and fish stock	lemon juice

1 Put the fish into a fireproof dish with salt, pepper, squeeze of lemon juice, butter and a little milk. Cover and bake in a moderate oven (350°F – Gas Mark 4), for about 15–20 minutes.

2 When cooked, remove to a serving dish and keep hot.

3 Make the liquor up to ¾ pint with milk and use to make a sauce with the butter and flour.

4 Remove the yolks from the hard-boiled eggs. Chop the whites, add to the sauce. Season with salt, pepper and lemon juice.

5 Carefully stir in the egg yolk which has been rubbed through a sieve.

6 Pour some of the sauce over the fish and serve the rest separately.

7 Garnish with lemon and parsley.

Baked hake

cooking time: 20–25 minutes

you will need for 4 servings:

4 steaks of hake	lemon juice
1 onion, peeled and finely chopped	salt and pepper
	2–3 oz. butter
1 egg yolk	chopped parsley

1 Put the fish into a greased fireproof dish.

2 Sprinkle the onion on top.

3 Beat the egg yolk, add lemon to taste, salt and pepper and pour over the fish.

4 Dot each steak with butter, cover and bake in a moderate oven (350°F – Gas Mark 4) about 20 minutes.

5 Put the fish on to a serving dish. Pour the liquor into a small pan. Add the rest of the butter a little at a time. Make quite hot and pour over the fish.

6 Sprinkle with parsley before serving.

Fillet of sole tartare

cooking time: 25 minutes

you will need for 4 servings:

4 fillets of sole*	little milk
lemon juice	seasoning
*Plaice may be used if preferred	

For the tartare sauce:

1 packet savoury white sauce mix	2 teaspoons chopped capers
½ pint milk	lemon juice
1 egg yolk	cayenne pepper
1 tablespoon cream	salt
1 teaspoon chopped parsley	1½ tablespoons mayonnaise
2 teaspoons chopped gherkin	
	lemon wedges

1 Wash and skin the fillets and place in a baking dish.

2 Sprinkle with lemon juice and add a little milk and seasoning.

3 Bake in a moderate oven (350°F – Gas Mark 4) for 15–20 minutes.

4 Remove the fish from the liquid. Arrange the fillets on a hot dish. Keep warm.

5 Make up the sauce as directed on the packet using ½ pint milk.

6 Remove from the heat and stir in the egg yolk and cream.

7 Add the remaining ingredients.

8 Pour over the fish, garnish with lemon wedges.

Sole surprise

cooking time: 7–10 minutes

you will need for 4 servings:

2 medium-sized sole, filleted	1 oz. seedless raisins
salt, pepper and lemon juice	½ oz. almonds, finely chopped
3 tablespoons chutney	egg and breadcrumbs
	fat for frying

1 Trim the fillets and sprinkle each with salt, pepper and lemon juice.

2 Mix the chutney, raisins and almonds and spread evenly on each fillet.

3 Roll up, sprinkle with flour and coat with egg and breadcrumbs.

4 Fry in deep fat until golden brown, drain well and serve with maître d'hôtel butter or hollandaise sauce (see pages 13 and 82).

Seafood surprise

cooking time: 25 minutes

you will need for 4 servings:

1 lb. runner beans *or*	½ pint milk
1 large packet frozen beans	1 lb. sole or plaice fillets
1 packet mushroom sauce	2 oz. cheese, grated
	2 tomatoes, sliced

1 Cook the beans in boiling, salted water until tender.

2 Make up the mushroom sauce according to the instructions on the packet, using ½ pint milk.

3 Cut the fillets into convenient sized pieces and arrange on top of the drained beans in a buttered baking dish. Pour the mushroom sauce over the fish and grill under medium heat for 10–15 minutes.

4 Sprinkle the cheese on top and arrange the tomato slices over the cheese.

5 Cook for a further 5 minutes under a hot grill until golden brown.

Stuffed herrings

cooking time: about 20 minutes

you will need for 4 servings:

4 fresh herrings with soft roe	squeeze garlic juice
1 tablespoon chopped parsley	4 tablespoons breadcrumbs
1 tablespoon finely chopped onion	1 hard-boiled egg
	salt and pepper
	milk

1 Prepare the fish, remove the roe and the backbone and open out the fish.

2 Mix all the other ingredients with the roe, season carefully and moisten with a little milk.

3 Spread on half the herring and cover with the other half.

4 Move carefully into a fireproof dish and bake in a moderate oven (350°F – Gas Mark 4) for about 20 minutes.

5 Serve with wedges of lemon.

Grilled herring gratinée

cooking time: 10–15 minutes

you will need for 4 servings:

4 fresh herrings	1 tablespoon chopped shallot
2 tablespoons oil	2 tomatoes, peeled and chopped
1 tablespoon chopped parsley	salt and pepper
2–3 chives, chopped	

1 Prepare the herrings and remove the roes.

2 Mix the roe with the oil, parsley, shallot, chives and tomatoes. Season and cook all together in a small pan, stirring well for about 3 minutes.

3 Grill the herrings and put into a fireproof dish. Pour the sauce over and if liked brown under the grill.

Danish herrings

cooking time: about 10 minutes to fry

you will need for 4 servings:

4 fresh herrings	1 large onion, peeled and cut into rings
fat for frying	
3–4 tablespoons vinegar	1 teaspoon brown sugar
6–8 peppercorns	

1 Prepare and bone the herrings. Fry in the usual way, or grill, and put aside to cool.

2 Mix the vinegar, onion rings, peppercorns and sugar together.

3 Put in the herrings and leave to marinate.

4 Serve cold, decorated with onion rings and serve thickly sliced beetroot separately.

Baked mackerel

cooking time: 20–25 minutes

you will need for 4 servings:

4 mackerel	4 tablespoons white wine
2 oz. butter	*bouquet garni*
salt and pepper	1 tablespoon chopped parsley
little French mustard	

1 Prepare the mackerel and put into a fireproof dish with the butter.

2 Season with salt and pepper and spread a little mustard over each fish.

3 Pour over the wine, put in the *bouquet garni* and bake in a moderate oven (350°F – Gas Mark 4).

4 Before serving, remove the *bouquet garni* and sprinkle with parsley.

17

Mackerel with horseradish sauce

cooking time: 15 minutes

you will need for 4 servings:

4 mackerel	2 tablespoons grated
1 oz. butter	horseradish
¾ oz. cornflour	salt and pepper
2 cartons yoghourt	parsley to garnish
vinegar to taste	

1 Prepare the mackerel, brush with a little oil and grill in the usual way.
2 Melt the butter in a pan, add the cornflour and mix well.
3 Add the yoghourt and stir until boiling. Simmer until it thickens slightly.
4 Add horseradish, vinegar to taste and salt and pepper.
5 Serve the mackerel garnished with parsley and hand the sauce separately.

Trout en papillote

cooking time: about 20 minutes

you will need for 4 servings:

1 trout per person	salt and pepper
lemon juice	
For garnish:	
1 oz. almonds,	lemon
browned and	
shredded	

1 Prepare some squares of aluminium foil (one for each trout) by brushing over with oil or melted butter.
2 Wash and dry the fish and lay on the foil.
3 Sprinkle with lemon juice, salt and pepper.
4 Fold the foil over the fish covering it completely. Put into a baking tin and cook about 20 minutes in a moderate oven (350°F – Gas Mark 4).
5 Carefully unwrap each fish and serve with its own juice. Sprinkle with almonds and garnish with wedges of lemon.

Stuffed whiting

cooking time: 20–25 minutes

you will need for 4 servings:

2 whiting	grated rind ½ lemon
4 oz. fresh	1 tablespoon chopped
breadcrumbs	parsley
1 oz. butter	1 egg
1 oz. walnuts,	salt and pepper
chopped	

1 Prepare the fish, split and remove the back-bone.
2 Reserve 2 tablespoons of the breadcrumbs and mix the rest with the butter, walnuts, lemon rind and parsley.
3 Bind with a little egg and season carefully.
4 Spread the filling on one half of the fish and cover with the other. Brush over with a little melted butter or oil. Cover with greaseproof paper and bake about 20 minutes in a moderate oven (350°F – Gas Mark 4).
5 Fry the remaining breadcrumbs in a little butter and sprinkle on top of the fish before serving.

Cheesy fish pie

cooking time: 25 minutes

you will need for 4 servings:

1 lb. cod fillets	½ teaspoon dry mustard
2 oz. butter	1 packet mashed
½ pint milk	potato
salt and pepper	3 oz. grated Cheddar
1 hard-boiled egg	cheese
1 oz. cornflour	

1 Simmer the cod fillets gently in the butter and milk, until tender, with a sprinkling of salt and pepper.
2 Remove from the pan and place in a flame-proof dish, with the egg chopped roughly.
3 Blend the cornflour and mustard with a little of the milk. Stir into the pan containing milk and butter and bring to the boil. Boil for 1 minute. Pour over the fish.
4 Make up the potato according to the instructions on the packet. Spread over the fish.
5 Sprinkle with grated cheese and warm through in the oven at 400°F Gas Mark 6, or under the grill.

To use cooked fish

Hake au gratin

cooking time: 15–20 minutes

you will need for 4 servings:

8 oz. cooked hake	2 oz. grated cheese
1 4-oz. can shrimps	2 bananas
½ pint white sauce	lemon juice
(see page 21)	little butter
1 egg	

1 Flake the fish, removing all skin and bone.

2 Add the shrimps, reserving a few for garnish.

3 Make the white sauce, cool a little, then add the yolk of egg and half the cheese.

4 Whisk the egg white stiffly and fold into the sauce.

5 Put the fish into a fireproof dish and pour the sauce over.

6 Sprinkle with the remaining cheese and dot with butter.

7 Bake in a moderate oven (350°F – Gas Mark 4) for about 15 minutes.

8 Slice the bananas, brush with lemon juice and a little melted butter.

9 Arrange round the edge of the dish and return to the oven for a further 5 minutes.

Fish puffs

cooking time: 5–10 minutes

you will need for 4 servings:

8 oz. cooked white fish	2 teaspoons anchovy essence
salt and pepper	2 eggs
lemon juice	1 oz. flour
	fat, deep for frying

1 Flake the fish very finely, removing all skin and bone.

2 Season very carefully and add lemon juice and anchovy essence.

3 Add the egg yolks and the flour and beat until the mixture is creamy.

4 Fold in the stiffly beaten egg whites.

5 Drop spoonfuls into hot fat and fry until crisp and well puffed.

6 Drain and serve with devilled sauce (see page 22).

Fish and potato pie

cooking time: 20 minutes

you will need for 4 servings:

1 oz. butter	2 tomatoes, peeled and chopped
½ small onion, chopped finely	2 oz. grated cheese
1 oz. flour	1 lb. cooked white fish
½ pint milk	lemon juice or vinegar
salt and pepper	1 lb. mashed potatoes
1 teaspoon tomato purée	

1 Melt the butter, add the onion, cook until soft but not coloured.

2 Add the flour and mix well.

3 Remove from the heat, add the milk and stir well. Return to the heat, stir until boiling and cook for 3 minutes.

4 Add seasoning, tomato purée, tomatoes and grated cheese.

5 Add the fish and correct the seasoning, adding lemon juice or vinegar as required.

6 Pour into a fireproof dish and cover with the mashed potato.

7 Brush over with a little milk and put into a moderately hot oven (375°F – Gas Mark 5) to brown.

Kedgeree

cooking time: about 15 minutes

you will need for 4 servings:

4 oz. Patna rice	salt and pepper
12 oz. cooked smoked haddock	cayenne pepper
	milk
2 oz. butter	1 teaspoon chopped parsley
1 egg	
1 hard-boiled egg	

1 Boil the rice in salted water for 12 minutes, then drain.

2 Add the flaked fish, butter, beaten egg, chopped white from the hard-boiled egg and seasoning.

3 Heat all thoroughly and add a little milk if the mixture is too dry.

4 Pile on to a hot dish and decorate with the sieved hard-boiled egg yolk and chopped parsley.

Savoury fish custard

cooking time: about 30 minutes

you will need for 4 servings:

8 oz. cooked smoked haddock	½ pint milk
3 eggs	salt and pepper
3 level teaspoons cornflour	1 teaspoon chopped parsley or a pinch mixed herbs

1 Flake the fish very finely and put it into a greased fireproof dish.

2 Mix the eggs smoothly with the cornflour, add the milk gradually and beat all well together.

3 Add seasoning and parsley and pour over the fish.

4 Bake in a moderately hot oven (375°F – Gas Mark 5).

Fish cutlets

cooking time: about 10 minutes

you will need for 4 servings:

8 oz. cooked white fish	lemon juice
2 oz. butter	1 teaspoon anchovy essence
2 oz. flour	egg and breadcrumbs
½ pint milk	fat, for deep frying
salt and pepper	

1 Flake the fish and remove all skin and bone.
2 Make a sauce with butter, flour and milk.
3 Add salt, pepper, lemon juice and anchovy essence.
4 Add the fish and mix thoroughly.
5 Spread on to a wetted plate and leave to become cold.
6 Divide into equal portions and shape into cutlets.
7 Coat with egg and breadcrumbs and fry in hot fat.
8 Drain well and serve with lemon and parsley.

Russian fish pie

cooking time: 20–25 minutes

you will need for 4 servings:

8 oz. flaky or rough puff pastry (see page 86)	1 dessertspoon chopped capers
12 oz. cooked white fish	1 hard-boiled egg, chopped
1 tablespoon chopped parsley	little white sauce seasoning

1 Roll the pastry into a square shape, trim the edges and keep for decoration.
2 Flake the fish and mix it with the parsley, capers and hard-boiled egg.
3 Moisten with a little white sauce and season.
4 Put the fish into the centre of the pastry. Damp the edges and fold the corners to the centre, enclosing the fish. Press the edges well together and decorate with the trimmings of pastry.
5 Brush over with egg or milk and bake about 20 minutes in a hot oven (425°F – Gas Mark 7).

Spaghetti Italiano

cooking time: 10 minutes

you will need for 3 servings:

6 oz. spaghetti	7-oz. can tuna fish
1 packet tomato soup	2 oz. grated cheese
¾ pint water	

1 Cook the spaghetti in boiling, salted water until tender. Drain well, turn into a hot dish.
2 Make up the tomato soup as directed on the packet using ¾ pint water.
3 Drain and flake the tuna fish.
4 Add to the soup and pour over the spaghetti.
5 Sprinkle with cheese and serve.

Baked fish pudding

cooking time: 20–25 minutes

you will need for 4 servings:

1 lb. cooked white fish	grated rind 1 lemon
3 oz. breadcrumbs	salt and pepper
2 eggs	lemon juice
little onion, finely chopped	1 oz. grated cheese
1 tablespoon milk	½ oz. butter

1 Remove all skin and bone from the fish and flake finely.
2 Add the breadcrumbs except for 1 tablespoon.
3 Add the eggs, beaten up with the milk, onion, lemon rind, salt and pepper.
4 Add lemon juice to taste and a little extra milk if the mixture is too dry.
5 Put into a greased fireproof dish, sprinkle with the remaining breadcrumbs and cheese, dot with butter and bake in a moderately hot oven (375°F – Gas Mark 5) for about 20 minutes.

Fish soufflé pie

cooking time: about 25 minutes

you will need for 4 servings:

6 oz. cooked white fish	1 tablespoon thin cream
1 oz. butter	salt and pepper
¾ oz. cornflour	lemon juice
¼ pint milk	1 dessertspoon finely chopped parsley
2 eggs	
1 tablespoon breadcrumbs	

1 Flake the fish very finely.
2 Make a thick white sauce with the butter, cornflour and milk.
3 Add egg yolks, fish, breadcrumbs, cream, seasoning, lemon juice and parsley.
4 Fold in the stiffly beaten egg white.
5 Put into a greased pie dish and bake in a moderately hot oven (375°F – Gas Mark 5) for about 20–25 minutes.

Sardine snack

cooking time: 10 minutes

you will need for 4 servings:

4 slices bread	salt and pepper
a little butter	1 packet cheese
1 tin sardines	sauce
1 tablespoon vinegar	½ pint milk

1 Toast bread on both sides.
2 Remove crusts and spread lightly with butter. Cut bread into fingers.
3 Drain sardines and arrange 1 or 2 on each piece of bread. Sprinkle with vinegar, salt and pepper.
4 Place on flameproof dish and keep warm under grill.
5 Make up cheese sauce according to instructions on the packet using ½ pint milk and pour over sardines.
6 Brown under grill and serve.

Tuna cheese bake

cooking time: 15 minutes

you will need for 2–3 servings:

3 small tomatoes	7-oz. can tuna fish
1 packet cheese sauce	1 small can sweet corn
½ pint milk	
To garnish:	
small packet plain potato crisps	2 oz. coarsely grated cheese

1 Slice tomatoes and place in bottom of fireproof dish.
2 Make sauce according to instructions on packet using ½ pint milk.
3 Add flaked tuna fish, and drained sweet corn, pour over tomatoes.
4 Lightly crush the potato crisps and mix with grated cheese, sprinkle over sauce.
5 Heat through in a hot oven (400°F – Gas Mark 6) for 10 minutes or brown under the grill.
6 Serve hot or cold with salad.

Salmon crunch

cooking time: 5 minutes

you will need for 2 servings:

4¾-oz. can red salmon	2–3 tablespoons corn
5 level tablespoons mayonnaise	oil
salt and pepper	2 slices white bread diced
pinch nutmeg	lettuce and cucumber

1 Drain the liquid from the can of salmon and remove any skin and bones.

2 Flake the salmon and add the mayonnaise and seasoning.
3 Heat the corn oil and fry the diced bread until crisp and golden brown. Drain well on kitchen paper and allow to become cold.
4 Add the fried bread to the salmon mixture just before serving.
5 Serve with a salad of lettuce and sliced cucumber.

Seafood vol-au-vents

cooking time: 10 minutes

you will need:

6 large vol-au-vent cases	4-oz. packet frozen prawns, defrosted
1 packet parsley sauce mix	1 tablespoon white wine
½ pint milk	fresh parsley
1 tin crab, drained and flaked	

1 Put vol-au-vent cases in a hot oven to warm through.
2 Make up the sauce as directed on the packet, using ½ pint milk.
3 Stir in the crab, prawns and white wine. Heat the mixture through and fill the vol-au-vent cases.
4 Garnish each case with a sprig of fresh parsley and serve.

Sauces to serve with fish

Basic white sauce

cooking time: about 10 minutes

you will need:

½ oz. butter	½ pint milk or milk and
½ oz. cornflour	fish stock
salt and pepper	lemon juice

1 Melt the butter, add the cornflour and mix well
2 Draw away from the heat, add the liquid, stir well.
3 Return to the heat, stir till boiling and boil for 3 minutes.
4 Add seasoning and lemon juice as required.

Anchovy sauce: To ½ pint basic white sauce add 2–3 teaspoons anchovy essence.

Cheese sauce: To ½ pint basic white sauce add 2–3 oz. grated cheese.

Egg sauce: To ½ pint basic white sauce add 1 chopped hard-boiled egg.

Fennel sauce: To ½ pint basic white sauce add 2 tablespoons chopped fennel.

Maître d'hôtel sauce: To ½ pint basic white sauce add 1 tablespoon finely chopped parsley and mix well. Add two teaspoons lemon juice and two tablespoons thin cream or evaporated milk.

Mustard sauce: To ½ pint basic white sauce add 2 level teaspoons dry mustard mixed with 2 teaspoons vinegar.

Parsley sauce: To ½ pint basic white sauce add 1–2 tablespoons finely chopped parsley.

Hollandaise sauce: See recipe on page 82.

Devilled sauce

cooking time: about 5 minutes

you will need for 4 servings:

3 tablespoons redcurrant jelly	1 tablespoon made mustard
few olives	1 gherkin

1 Heat the jelly in a small pan.
2 Add the mustard and mix well.
3 Add the olives, sliced thinly and the gherkin finely chopped.

Meat Dishes

When you are really hungry there is nothing more satisfying than a savoury and delicious main course of hot meat and vegetables. And there is no reason why the preparation of such dishes need be either complicated or time-consuming. In the following chapter you will find a great variety of recipes guaranteed to satisfy the most demanding appetites. And they are all both quick and easy to prepare.

Fried steak and onions

cooking time: 20 minutes

you will need for 4 servings:

3–4 onions	1½ lb. rump steak
2 oz. dripping	salt and pepper

1 Peel onions and slice into rings a good ⅛ inch thick.
2 Heat dripping and fry onions over a gentle heat until dark golden brown, turning frequently while cooking.
3 Remove from the pan, drain on crushed kitchen paper and keep hot.
4 Prepare steak as for grilled steak. Fry for 10–15 minutes turning the steak when browned on the first side.
5 Serve steaks on a hot plate with onions piled on top.

Grilled steak

cooking time: 6–15 minutes, depending on cut

you will need for 4 servings:

1½ lb. steak cut ½–¾ inch thick	salt and pepper
lemon juice	maître d'hôtel butter (see page 13)
butter or oil	

1 Choose fillet, entrecôte or rump steak for grilling.
2 Prick with a fork all over and sprinkle with lemon juice.
3 Beat with a rolling pin, sprinkle with salt and pepper.
4 Brush with melted butter or oil.
5 Grease the rack of the grill pan and place steaks on the rack.
6 Cook under a hot grill until steak has browned slightly on first side.
7 Turn meat over, using a fish slice or palette knife to avoid piercing the steak.
8 Cook quickly until brown on the second side.
9 Allow 6–10 minutes for fillet steak, 10–15 minutes for entrecôte, 10–15 for rump steak.
10 Serve steak on a hot meat dish, top each with a pat of maître d'hôtel butter.
11 The usual accompaniments for grilled steak are grilled tomatoes or mushrooms, chipped potatoes and watercress.

Steak Milano

cooking time: about 15 minutes
(prepare the day before)

you will need for 4 servings:

1½ lb. rump steak, cut ½ inch thick	juice ½ lemon
2 cloves garlic	salt and pepper
⅓ pint oil	1 large packet frozen spinach

1 Trim steak, cutting off excess fat, if necessary.
2 Chop garlic finely and mix with oil, lemon juice and salt and pepper.
3 Allow the steaks to soak in this mixture for at least 12 hours.
4 Grill the steaks as described in Grilled steak, opposite. Serve with cooked spinach.

Steak royale

cooking time: 15 minutes

you will need for 4 servings:

8 oz. button mushrooms	salt and pepper
2 oz. butter	2 tablespoons chopped parsley
1 clove garlic	1 carton cultured cream
1½ lb. rump steak cut ½ inch thick	

1 Peel mushrooms if necessary, cook in melted butter over a gentle heat for 10 minutes, adding the garlic, finely chopped.
2 Brush steaks with a little melted butter and cook as described in the previous recipe.
3 Add the parsley to the mushrooms, cook for 2–3 minutes longer, stir in the cream.
4 Pour the mushroom mixture over the steak and serve accompanied by French bread and a green salad.

Steak fondue

cooking time: about 20 minutes

you will need for 4 servings:

1½ lb. rump steak	paprika pepper
4 oz. Lancashire or Cheddar cheese	mustard
3–4 tablespoons sherry	broccoli or mushrooms for serving
salt	

1 Prepare steak and grill or fry as described in previous recipes.
2 Meanwhile, heat cheese in a basin over a pan of hot water until the cheese has melted.
3 Gradually add the sherry, stirring throughout.
4 Season to taste with salt, pepper and mustard.

5 Pour cheese over the steak and serve, accompanied with cooked broccoli or mushrooms.

Scandinavian steakburgers

cooking time: 8–10 minutes

you will need for 4 servings:

2 oz. butter	1 large packet steakburgers
2 oz. Danish blue cheese	

1 Cream the butter and blend with the cheese. Leave in a cool place until required.
2 Grill the steakburgers until tender.
3 Place on a hot dish and top each with a pat of the butter mixture.
4 Garnish with watercress and serve with French fried potatoes.

Beefburger special

cooking time: 20 minutes

you will need for 4 servings:

1 lb. raw minced beef	salt and pepper
2 oz. fresh breadcrumbs (4 heaped tablespoons)	1 beaten egg flour
1 medium-sized onion, finely chopped	oil or fat for frying 4 eggs
2 teaspoons chopped parsley	

1 Mix the beef, breadcrumbs, onion and parsley, adding a good pinch of salt and pepper.
2 Bind together with beaten egg.
3 Turn on to a floured surface. Divide mixture into 8 portions.
4 Form into 8 cakes using floured hands.
5 Fry in hot oil or fat until browned on both sides and cooked through – about 15 minutes. Remove on to a hot dish.
6 Fry the eggs.
7 Serve each two beefburgers with a fried egg, and accompanied by tomato sauce or sweet chutney.

Cheeseburgers: Prepare as above, omitting fried eggs. Top burgers with sliced raw tomato, pour thick cheese sauce (see page 83) over and brown under the grill if liked.

Lamburgers: Prepare as above using lamb in place of beef. Omit onion and fried eggs and serve with onion sauce (see page 83), accompanied by peas. Mint may be used in place of parsley.

Frankfurter and corn flan

cooking time: 30 minutes

you will need for 4 servings:

1 packet savoury white sauce	2 oz. grated cheese
½ pint milk	1 egg
7-oz. can whole corn niblets	baked pastry case
8-oz. can frankfurter sausages, sliced	

1 Make up the sauce as directed on the packet using ½ pint milk.
2 Stir in the corn niblets, the frankfurter sausages and the grated cheese.
3 Separate the egg and stir in the yolk.
4 Whisk the egg white until stiff and fold into the sauce mixture.
5 Turn into the pastry case. Bake at 400°F, Gas Mark 6 for 20 minutes. Serve hot or cold.

Meat balls

cooking time: 5–7 minutes

you will need for 4 servings:

1 lb. raw minced beef	2 slices bread
4 oz. sausage meat	¼ pint milk
2 medium-sized onions	salt and pepper
½ teaspoon grated lemon rind	2 eggs
	flour
1 teaspoon chopped parsley	browned breadcrumbs
	fat for frying

1 Mix the beef and sausage meat, adding the onions, grated or finely chopped, lemon rind and parsley.
2 Remove crusts from bread, soak slices in milk and mash to a paste with a fork.
3 Add bread, 1 egg and a good pinch salt and pepper to meat. Mix well.
4 Leave in a cold place for 2–3 hours.
5 Form into balls with floured hands. Dip in beaten egg, toss in breadcrumbs.
6 Fry in deep fat until golden brown. Drain well and serve.

Meat balls with noodles

cooking time: 45 minutes

you will need for 4 servings:

meat balls (see preceding recipe)	1 pint stock, made from beef stock cube
2 oz. butter	salt and pepper
2 tablespoons flour	8 oz. noodles

1 Make meat balls as in preceding recipe. Omit egg and breadcrumb coating.
2 Melt butter, stir in the flour and cook for 3 minutes.
3 Gradually stir in stock and bring to the boil. Reduce heat and simmer for 20 minutes, adding salt and pepper to taste.
4 Add meat balls, cover and cook over a low heat for 15 minutes.
5 Meanwhile, cook noodles in boiling salted water until tender. Drain well.
6 Pile noodles in a hot dish. Pour sauce and meat balls into the centre and serve.

Veal Luxembourg

cooking time: 20 minutes

you will need for 4 servings:

4 thin escalopes veal	2 tablespoons lemon juice
4 thin slices ham	2 tablespoons cream
2 oz. butter	
8 small mushrooms	

1 Fry the veal in butter until tender, remove to warm dish and keep hot.
2 Fry ham slices and place one slice on top of each escalope.
3 Fry mushrooms, adding more butter to the pan if necessary.
4 Arrange mushrooms in dish with veal and ham.
5 Heat cream and lemon juice in the pan, making sure that the mixture does not boil.
6 Pour over the veal and serve.

Veal à la Russe

cooking time: 6 minutes

you will require for 4 servings:

4 escalopes of veal	½ pint milk
salt and pepper	4 tablespoons sour cream
flour	
egg and breadcrumbs for coating	anchovy fillets (optional) or slices of lemon
2 tablespoons corn oil	
1 packet mushroom sauce mix	

1 Dip the escalopes in flour seasoned with salt and pepper, then in egg and breadcrumbs.
2 Fry escalopes in oil until tender – about 5 minutes.

3 Meanwhile, make up the sauce according to instructions on the packet.

4 Remove from the heat and stir in the cream.

5 Serve escalopes with sauce poured over, garnish with anchovy fillets or slices of lemon.

Veal à la Suisse: Prepare veal and sauce as above. Serve with boiled rice to which chopped cooked bacon and peas have been added.

Hawaiian pork patties

cooking time: 15–20 minutes

you will need for 4 servings:

8 oz. pork sausage meat	1 egg
4 tablespoons fresh breadcrumbs	browned breadcrumbs for coating
1 tablespoon chopped parsley or mint	oil for frying
cornflour	4 slices canned pineapple
salt and pepper	1 teaspoon French mustard

1 Mix sausage meat, breadcrumbs, parsley or mint.

2 Shape into 4 round cakes.

3 Coat with cornflour seasoned with salt and pepper.

4 Dip in egg and breadcrumbs.

5 Fry in hot oil until browned on both sides and cooked through.

6 Remove from pan and keep hot.

7 Drain pineapple rings. Smear lightly with mustard. Fry for 5 minutes.

8 Top each patty with a pineapple ring.

Gammon steaks with honey glaze

cooking time: 25 minutes approximately

you will need for 4 servings:

2 tablespoons corn oil	2 tablespoons vinegar
2 tablespoons honey	4 gammon steaks $\frac{1}{4}$–$\frac{1}{2}$ inch thick

1 Put the corn oil, honey and vinegar in a saucepan and bring to the boil.

2 Snip the fat around each gammon steak and brush with a little of the glaze.

3 Grill on one side of the steaks for 5–10 minutes then turn them over, brush again with the glaze and continue cooking for a further 5–10 minutes or until tender.

4 Serve with creamed potatoes.

Hawaiian gammon

cooking time: about 20 minutes

you will need for 4 servings:

1 oz. soft brown sugar	1-lb. can pineapple rings
1 level teaspoon dry mustard	juice 1 orange
4 rashers gammon	1 packet savoury white sauce mix
2 tablespoons corn oil	1 or 2 cloves (optional)

1 Mix sugar and mustard together, sprinkle over rashers and rub in well.

2 Fry the rashers on both sides until tender – about 10 minutes.

3 Drain juice from pineapple, add orange juice and make up to $\frac{1}{2}$ pint with water if necessary.

4 Make up the white sauce as directed on the packet, but use the $\frac{1}{2}$ pint fruit juice in place of milk.

5 Remove gammon from the pan, pour off excess oil.

6 Replace gammon in the pan, pour sauce over, add cloves if liked, and pineapple rings and cook for a further 5 minutes.

7 Serve with spinach and creamed potatoes.

Barbecued gammon steak

cooking time: 30 minutes

you will need for 4 servings:

1 thick slice gammon, about $\frac{3}{4}$ lb.	1 small onion
little corn oil	baked bananas and jacket potatoes, if liked
1 packet tomato soup	
$\frac{3}{4}$ pint water	
1 green pepper, thinly sliced	

1 Brush both sides of the gammon with a little corn oil. Grill very slightly on both sides.

2 Place on aluminium foil on a baking tray.

3 Make up the tomato soup as directed on the packet, using $\frac{3}{4}$ pint water. Pour over the gammon.

4 Top with pepper and sliced onion and fold over the foil so that the gammon is encased.

5 Bake in a hot oven (400°F – Gas Mark 6) for 25 minutes.

6 Serve with baked bananas and jacket potatoes.

Bacon and tomato grill

cooking time: about 13 minutes

you will need for 4 servings:

4 rashers back bacon	good pinch salt,
4 slices bread	pepper and castor
1 lb. tomatoes	sugar
1 level teaspoon	2 oz. cheese, finely
mixed herbs	grated
1 oz. butter	dripping or oil for
	frying

1 Remove rind from rashers and fry bacon for about 5 minutes. Remove and keep hot.
2 Add extra fat to the pan if necessary and fry the bread until crisp.
3 Meanwhile, skin and slice the tomatoes. Place in a shallow fireproof dish. Sprinkle with mixed herbs, salt, pepper and sugar.
4 Dot with butter, grill for about 5 minutes.
5 Sprinkle with cheese and grill for a further 3 minutes until golden.
6 Cover the fried bread with tomato mixture, top with bacon and serve.

Bacon apple grill

cooking time: 20 minutes

you will need for 4 servings:

4 gammon rashers	$\frac{1}{4}$ pint cider
8 oz. cheese, finely	1 large cooking apple
grated	1 oz. demerara sugar

1 Trim the fat off the bacon, cook under the grill until tender, turning rashers once during cooking.
2 Meanwhile, put the cheese into a saucepan with the cider and melt it over a very low heat, stirring all the time. After it has melted continue stirring until the mixture gradually thickens.
3 Peel and cut the apple into twelve sections, removing the core. Sprinkle sections lightly with the sugar and put them under a hot grill for a few minutes on each side to heat and lightly caramelise them.
4 Serve the bacon rashers garnished with apple and accompanied by cheese sauce and sauté or creamed potatoes.

Grilled ham and cheese rolls

cooking time: 15 minutes

you will need for 4 servings:

8 slices ham	oil
French mustard	4 pineapple rings
8 slices processed	4 slices buttered toast
cheese	watercress

1 Spread slices of ham with a little mustard. Top each slice of ham with a slice of cheese.
2 Roll up like a Swiss roll and secure each with a cocktail stick.
3 Brush each with oil and grill until cheese begins to melt. Remove from grill pan and keep hot.
4 Drain pineapple rings, brush with oil and grill for 5 minutes.
5 Place 1 pineapple ring on each piece of toast, top each with two ham rolls and garnish with watercress.

Ham Napoli: Prepare ham rolls (see above) and serve with boiled rice and tomato sauce (see page 83).

Pork chops country style

cooking time: 20 minutes

you will need for 4 servings:

4 loin chops	fresh breadcrumbs
1 egg	1½ oz. butter
1 teaspoon powdered	apple sauce (see page
sage	83)
salt and pepper	

1 Trim the chops, removing as much fat as possible.
2 Beat the egg, add sage and a pinch of salt and pepper.
3 Coat each chop with egg and breadcrumbs.
4 Fry in butter, turning frequently, until golden brown and tender.
5 Serve with apple sauce and creamed potato.

Barbecued lamb

cooking time: 20 minutes

you will need for 4 servings:

6 oz. long grained rice	4 tablespoons red
1 oz. butter	currant jelly
1 dessertspoon	seasoning
vinegar	8 oz. cooked lamb
$\frac{1}{4}$ teaspoon dry	1 small packet frozen
mustard	peas

1 Cook the rice in boiling salted water for about 12 minutes.
2 Meanwhile, melt the butter and add the vinegar, red currant jelly and mustard.
3 Heat through and season to taste with salt and pepper.
4 Cut the lamb into cubes, add to sauce and heat through for about 10 minutes.
5 Cook peas as directed on the packet.
6 Drain the rice, rinse and drain again.
7 Mix rice and peas, place in a hot dish, pile lamb in the centre and serve.

Braised pork chops

cooking time: about 30 minutes

you will need for 4 servings:

4 pork chops (cut 1 inch thick)	oil for drying
cornflour	1 onion (optional)
salt and pepper	2 tablespoons tomato juice

1 Trim chops and coat with cornflour, seasoned with salt and pepper.
2 Choose a pan big enough to take the chops in a single layer.
3 Pour in sufficient oil to cover the bottom of the pan.
4 Add chops and brown on both sides.
5 Pour in tomato juice. Add onion thinly sliced.
6 Cover and simmer until chops are tender.
7 Serve with creamed potatoes.

Liver country style

cooking time: 30 minutes

you will need for 2–3 servings:

8 oz. lamb's liver, sliced	$\frac{1}{2}$ pint milk
2 tablespoons corn oil	2 oz. mushrooms, sliced
1 packet onion sauce	

1 Fry liver in oil, then drain and place in oven-proof casserole.
2 Make sauce according to directions on packet using $\frac{1}{2}$ pint milk. Pour over liver.
3 Cover and bake at 350°F, Gas Mark 4 for about 25 minutes.
4 Add mushrooms 15 minutes before end of cooking.

Liver continental style

cooking time: 15 minutes

you will need for 4 servings:

1 lb. calf's liver	2 rashers back bacon
cornflour	1 small onion
seasoning	$\frac{1}{2}$ lemon
1 oz. butter	8 oz. boiled Patna rice

1 Slice liver $\frac{1}{2}$ inch thick, coat with cornflour seasoned with salt and pepper.
2 Fry liver in melted butter, 3–4 minutes each side.
3 Remove from pan, keep hot.
4 Fry bacon until just crisp, keep hot.
5 Slice onion thinly, cook until brown in fat remaining in pan.
6 Add 3 tablespoons hot water and bring to the boil. Season to taste.
7 Sprinkle liver with lemon juice.
8 Arrange bacon on rice, place liver on top and pour onion gravy over.

Kidney and bacon de luxe

cooking time: about 20 minutes

you will need for 4 servings:

2 sheep's kidneys	2 large tomatoes
2 rashers bacon	4 slices toast
2 oz. butter	salt and pepper
4 oz. mushrooms	sugar
4 eggs	

1 Skin kidneys, remove the core and soak in cold water for 5 minutes.
2 Chop kidneys and bacon, fry in 1 oz. butter for 5 minutes over a gentle heat.
3 Chop mushrooms, add to kidney and bacon with remaining butter as required. Fry gently for a further 5 minutes.
4 Remove from pan and keep hot. Fry eggs.
5 Cut tomatoes in thick slices, sprinkle with a little salt, pepper and sugar. Fry lightly.
6 Spread mushroom mixture over each slice of toast. Top each with a fried egg and garnish with sliced tomato.

Lamb cutlets with spinach

cooking time: 20 minutes

you will need for 4 servings:

8 lamb cutlets	2 tablespoons thin
1 egg	cream or top of the
salt and pepper	milk
breadcrumbs	nutmeg
1 oz. butter	
1 large packet frozen	
spinach	

1 Trim cutlets, brush with beaten egg sprinkled with salt and pepper.
2 Coat cutlets with breadcrumbs. Fry quickly in melted butter until browned on both sides. Reduce heat and continue cooking until tender.
3 Cook spinach as directed on the packet.
4 Stir in cream or milk and a good pinch grated nutmeg.
5 Pile spinach in the centre of a hot dish, arrange cutlets round and serve.

Lamb cutlets pascale

cooking time: 30 minutes

you will need for 4 servings:

3 onions	2 tablespoons Patna
2 tablespoons corn	rice
oil	$\frac{1}{4}$ pint stock
	8 lamb cutlets

Mornay sauce:

2 packets white sauce	6 oz. grated cheese
mix	1 egg yolk
$\frac{3}{4}$ pint milk	1 packet frozen peas

1 Chop the onions and sauté in the oil.
2 Add the rice and mix well. Add the stock, cover with greaseproof paper and a lid and cook gently for 20–30 minutes.
3 Trim the cutlets and fry in corn oil for 10 minutes. Remove and drain. Place on a serving dish and pile the onion mixture on top.
4 Place sauce mix in a pan and blend it with the milk. Bring to the boil stirring all the time. Boil for 1 minute.
5 Stir in the grated cheese and egg yolk.
6 Coat each cutlet with the Mornay Sauce and garnish with peas.

Kebabs with corn

cooking time: 8–10 minutes

you will need for 4 servings:

4 small tomatoes	2 oz. butter
8 small mushrooms	1 can sweet corn
4 rashers streaky	niblets
bacon	$\frac{1}{2}$ oz. butter
4 chipolata sausages	
8 small pieces cooked	
meat	

1 Cut the tomatoes in half, peel the mushrooms if necessary. Remove the rind from the bacon, cut each rasher in half and roll up making 8 bacon rolls. Prick the sausages, twist the centre of each and cut through making 8 small sausages.
2 Thread tomato, mushrooms, bacon rolls, sausages and pieces of meat alternately on to 4 8-inch skewers. Brush well with melted butter.
3 Cook under a hot grill turning the skewers at intervals so that all the ingredients are cooked evenly, brushing again with butter during cooking.
4 Meanwhile, heat the corn in a small pan, drain, add the $\frac{1}{2}$ oz. butter. Toss the corn and turn into a hot dish.
5 Place the skewers on the corn and serve.

With luncheon meat: Cubes of luncheon meat and pineapple may be used to make kebabs.

Curry pasties

cooking time: 15 minutes

you will need for 4 servings:

4 oz. cooked meat,	$\frac{1}{2}$ pint curry sauce
chopped	(see page 83)
3 oz. cooked rice	8 oz. flaky pastry (see
2 hard-boiled eggs,	page 86)
chopped	beaten egg for glazing
2 teaspoons chutney	

1 Mix together meat, rice, eggs and chutney with sufficient sauce to give a moist consistency.
2 Roll out pastry $\frac{1}{8}$ inch thick and cut into 4-inch squares.
3 Place a spoonful of filling in each square. Moisten edges of pastry with water or egg.
4 Fold corner into the centre to form an envelope.
5 Brush with egg and place on a baking tray.
6 Bake in a very hot oven (475°F – Gas Mark 8) until golden.

Super supper

cooking time: 20 minutes

you will need for 4 servings:

8 oz. streaky bacon	4 eggs
1 lb. boiled potatoes	1 oz. butter
1 small onion	4 oz. Cheddar cheese,
1 small green pepper	grated
salt and pepper	

1 Chop the bacon and fry gently. Remove from the pan.
2 Dice the potato, chop the onion and pepper. Cook in the bacon fat until lightly browned.
3 Turn into a flame-proof dish, with the bacon, and keep hot. Season.
4 Fry the eggs in the butter. Place on top of the potato mixture. Cover with grated cheese and brown under the grill.

Speedy layer pie

cooking time: 30 minutes

you will need for 4 servings:

1 lb. potatoes	8 oz. corned beef
4 small tomatoes	1 small packet frozen
1 large onion	mixed vegetables
2 oz. mushrooms	1 egg
2 oz. butter	milk

1 Cut potatoes into quarters and cook in boiling salted water until tender.
2 Sauté tomatoes, onion and mushrooms in 1 oz. butter.
3 Chop or slice corned beef. Cook the vegetables and drain.
4 Drain the potatoes, cream with the remaining butter, the egg (saving 1 tablespoon for glazing) and the milk.
5 Put a layer of potato in the bottom of a greased pie dish.
6 Arrange corned beef, tomato mixture and mixed vegetables in layers on top of the potato. Cover with remaining potato.
7 Mark potatoes with the back of a fork and brush with beaten egg.
8 Bake in a hot oven (450°F – Gas Mark 7) for 15 minutes until golden brown.

Bacon and egg flan

cooking time: 40 minutes

you will need for 4 servings:

6 oz. short crust	salt and pepper
pastry (see page 86)	½ teaspoon dry mustard
2 eggs	1 small can
6 rashers	evaporated milk
streaky bacon	2 tomatoes (optional)
3 oz. cheese	

1 Line an 8-inch pie plate with the pastry.
2 Beat the eggs. Remove the rind from the bacon and chop. Add to the beaten eggs with the grated cheese, salt, pepper and mustard.
3 Stir in the milk and pour the mixture into the pastry-lined plate.
4 Bake on the centre shelf of a moderately hot oven (375°F – Gas Mark 5).
5 When cooked and golden, remove from the oven and garnish with slices of tomato.

Ham and mushroom flan

cooking time: 10 minutes

you will need for 4 servings:

8-inch cooked pastry case	1 packet mushroom
2 hard-boiled eggs,	sauce
sliced	½ pint milk
4 oz. cooked ham,	1 oz. grated cheese
diced	

1 To make flan case see page 87. Arrange the sliced egg over the bottom of the flan case, keeping a few slices for garnish. Arrange diced ham on top of egg.
2 Make up the mushroom sauce as directed on the packet with ½ pint milk and pour over the ham.
3 Sprinkle with grated cheese and brown under a hot grill. Serve at once.

Meat patties

cooking time: 25 minutes

you will need for 4 servings:

1 lb. finely chopped	4 large cooked
cooked meat	potatoes
1 egg	4 tomatoes
browned breadcrumbs	seasoning
dripping	parsley
1 large onion	

1 Season the meat and bind with egg.
2 Form into small rounds, toss in breadcrumbs and fry in dripping until brown. Keep hot.
3 Peel and chop the onion and tomatoes.
4 Dice the potatoes and mix with the onion and tomato. *continued*

5 Fry gently until cooked, adding a little dripping to the pan as necessary.

6 Arrange in a warm dish. Top with the meat patties and serve.

Monday lunch

cooking time: about 30 minutes

you will need for 4 servings:

1 lb. cold cooked lamb	1 tablespoon cornflour
1 large onion	½ pint stock
1 oz. butter	4 oz. tomatoes
	salt and pepper

1 Slice meat, removing fat if necessary. Chop onion finely.

2 Melt butter, add onion, cook over a gentle heat for 5 minutes.

3 Blend in the cornflour, gradually stir in the stock, bring to the boil.

4 Reduce the heat. Add the tomatoes, skinned and chopped, simmer for 15 minutes.

5 Season to taste, add lamb, cover and cook for a further 10 minutes.

6 Serve with creamed potatoes.

Left-over lunch

cooking time: about 30 minutes

you will need for 4 servings:

2 oz. dripping	1–1½ lb. cooked meat
2 onions	(beef, pork or lamb)
4 large cooked chopped potatoes	cut into cubes
salt and pepper	mixed herbs
	4 eggs

1 Heat the dripping and fry the finely chopped onions until tender.

2 Add potato and cook until golden brown, add meat and season with salt, pepper and a pinch mixed herbs.

3 Cook until thoroughly heated, adding more fat if necessary to prevent the mixture from sticking to the pan.

4 Transfer to a shallow warmed dish.

5 Fry the eggs and place on top of the meat. Serve at once.

Chicken croquettes

cooking time: 15 minutes

you will need for 2 servings:

1 packet of bread sauce	Worcester sauce
½ pint milk	nutmeg
6 oz. cooked chicken, minced	corn oil for deep frying

For coating:

egg and breadcrumbs	1 level tablespoon cornflour

1 Make sauce as directed using ½ pint milk.

2 Stir in the chicken, Worcester sauce and a sprinkling of nutmeg.

3 Leave until cold then divide into 4 portions.

4 Coat with cornflour, then egg and crumbs.

5 Heat corn oil to 375°F. Fry croquettes until golden. Drain well and serve at once.

Chicken pilaff

cooking time: 30 minutes

you will need for 4 servings:

2 rashers bacon	¾ pint chicken stock
1 onion	2 oz. raisins
6 oz. Patna rice	1 green pepper
2 tablespoons oil	8 oz. cooked chicken
salt and pepper	

1 Remove the rind from bacon, chop roughly and fry in a large pan.

2 Chop onion, add with the oil to the bacon. Cook over a gentle heat for 5 minutes.

3 Add rice and cook for a further 5 minutes, stirring throughout with a fork.

4 Add stock, season to taste, add the raisins and pepper, chopped or cut into shreds.

5 Bring to the boil, reduce the heat, cover and simmer until the rice is tender and the stock is absorbed.

6 Chop chicken, stir into the rice. Cook for 5 minutes. Turn into a hot dish and serve.

Creamed chicken and asparagus

cooking time: 15 minutes

you will need for 4 servings:

1 packet asparagus soup	½ oz. cornflour
1¼ pints water	1 tablespoon milk
8 oz. cooked chicken and ham, chopped	¼ pint single cream
	1 egg yolk

To garnish:

bacon rolls and croûtes of fried bread

1 Make up the asparagus soup as directed on the packet using 1¼ pints of water. Stir in the chicken and ham.
2 Blend the cornflour smoothly with the milk, stir into the soup and cook for 5 minutes, stirring.
3 Blend the cream and egg yolk with a little of the hot soup. Stir back into the pan.
4 Pour into serving dish. Correct the seasoning.
5 Serve garnished with bacon rolls and croûtes of fried bread.

Chicken and peach bake

cooking time: 30 minutes

you will need for 4 servings:

1 lb. French beans or 1 large packet frozen beans, cooked	2 oz. Cheddar cheese, grated
2 oz. almonds, blanched	1 packet white sauce
8 oz. cooked chicken, sliced	½ pint milk
	1 can sliced peaches
	1 packet potato crisps

1 Arrange the beans, almonds, chicken and ¾ of the cheese in layers over the base of a large casserole.
2 Make up the white sauce as directed on the packet with ½ pint milk and pour over the ingredients in the casserole.
3 Bake in a moderate oven (350°F – Gas Mark 4) for 20 minutes.
4 Arrange the sliced peaches on the top of the dish, sprinkle with the remaining cheese and crushed crisps. Bake a further 10 minutes.

Oven fried chicken

cooking time: 15–20 minutes, depending on size of joint

you will need:

3–4 tablespoons corn oil	1 egg
4 chicken joints	4 tablespoons browned breadcrumbs
1 tablespoon seasoned flour	4 strips canned red pimento

1 Pour oil in roasting tin or shallow ovenproof dish. There should be sufficient to cover the bottom of the tin.
2 Put the dish into the oven at 375°F – Gas Mark 5, for 10 minutes to preheat oil.
3 Dip chicken joints in seasoned flour, then in egg and breadcrumbs, if wished.

4 Place joints in hot oil, baste well.
5 Bake uncovered until tender.
6 Drain on kitchen paper and garnish each one with a strip of red pimento.
With potato crisps: Potato crisps heated through in the oven and watercress make a good accompaniment to this dish.

Chicken curaçao

cooking time: 40 minutes

you will need for 4 servings:

2 tablespoons corn oil	1 small can mandarin oranges, drained
4 chicken joints, skinned and trimmed	¾ teaspoon tarragon vinegar
1 packet savoury white sauce mix	1 tablespoon curaçao
½ pint milk	peanuts

1 Heat the corn oil in a pan and fry the chicken joints lightly on both sides. Remove to a casserole.
2 Make up the white sauce mix as directed on the packet using ½ pint milk.
3 Stir in the mandarin orange juice, tarragon vinegar and curaçao. Pour the sauce over the chicken joints.
4 Cover and cook in a moderate oven (350°F – Gas Mark 4) for 25–30 minutes.
5 Add the mandarin oranges and sprinkle the top with peanuts.
6 Return to the oven for a further 10 minutes. Serve with plain boiled rice.

Festive chicken

cooking time: 20 minutes

you will need for 4 servings:

2 tablespoons corn oil	6 tablespoons cranberry sauce
1 can pimentos, chopped	12 oz. cooked chicken, cut into strips
1 medium onion	5 oz. water chestnuts, sliced
1 tablespoon cornflour	
½ pint chicken stock	

1 Heat the corn oil in a saucepan and lightly fry the pimentos and onion until soft.
2 Blend the cornflour with a little of the stock, pour with remaining stock and cranberries into the saucepan.
3 Bring to the boil, stirring constantly.
4 Add the chicken strips and water chestnuts and simmer for 5–7 minutes.
5 Serve with boiled rice.

Broccoli and chicken divan

cooking time: 30 minutes

you will need for 3 servings:

10-oz. carton green broccoli spears	1 packet savoury white sauce
2 oz. grated cheese	
8 oz. cooked diced chicken	

1 Cook the broccoli, drain well and place in a greased ovenproof dish. Sprinkle with a third of the cheese.
2 Add the diced chicken and sprinkle with a little more cheese.
3 Make up the white sauce and pour it over the chicken.
4 Sprinkle with the remaining cheese and heat through in the oven (350°F – Gas Mark 4) for 15–20 minutes.
5 To finish, brown under grill if liked.

Italian casserole

cooking time: 30 minutes

you will need for 4 servings:

2 oz. macaroni	1 pint boiling water
4 eggs	3 oz. grated cheese
1 oz. butter	4 oz. cooked ham or
1 oz. flour	bacon
1 chicken stock cube	buttered breadcrumbs

1 Cook macaroni until tender. Boil eggs for 10 minutes.
2 Melt butter in a pan, blend in flour and cook over a gentle heat for 3 minutes.
3 Dissolve the stock cube in boiling water, gradually stir into the flour and bring to the boil.
4 Reduce the heat and stir in the cheese.
5 Pour a little sauce into the bottom of a greased casserole, add half the macaroni, shelled eggs and ham chopped roughly. Cover with sauce, then with remaining macaroni.
6 Finish with sauce and sprinkle with breadcrumbs.
7 Bake in a moderate oven (350°F – Gas Mark 4) until the crumbs are well browned.

Country rice

cooking time: 25 minutes

you will need for 4 servings:

4 tablespoons corn oil	1½ pints water
8 oz. rice	2 oz. cooked ham
1 packet country vegetable soup	2 oz. mushrooms, sliced

1 Heat corn oil, add rice, sauté until golden.
2 Add the contents of the packet of soup and water, bring to the boil, stirring, cover and simmer for 10 minutes.
3 Stir in diced ham and mushrooms and continue cooking slowly until the liquid has been absorbed. This will take about 10 minutes.

Rice diablo

cooking time: about 15 minutes

you will need for 4 servings:

12 oz. long grained rice	1 small onion, finely grated
1 lb. liver sausage, unsliced	1 tablespoon mild mustard
3 oz. butter	4 tablespoons pineapple tidbits
1 tablespoon lemon juice	

1 Boil rice for 12 minutes in salted water.
2 Pour into colander, drain, rinse and drain again. Place colander over a pan of simmering water and steam until dry.
3 Remove skin from sausage and cut into 8 slices. Place in grill pan without the rack.
4 Blend butter with lemon, onion and mustard.
5 Spread over sausage and grill until browned and sizzling (about 5 minutes). Remove from grill pan and keep hot.
6 Drain pineapple, toss in the dripping in the pan, heat under a hot grill for 5 minutes.
7 To serve, mix pineapple with rice, pile into a hot dish and place the sausage on top.

Corned beef quickie

cooking time: 30 minutes

you will need for 4 servings:

12 oz. corned beef	8 oz. tomatoes
paprika pepper	1 beef stock cube
8 oz. cooked potatoes	¾ pint boiling water
1 onion	chopped parsley
1 can celery hearts	

1 Chop meat roughly, adding a pinch of paprika.
2 Slice potatoes, chop onion finely, drain and chop celery, skin and slice the tomatoes.

3 Arrange the ingredients in layers in a casserole.

4 Dissolve beef stock cube in boiling water, pour into casserole.

5 Cover and bake in a hot oven (425°F – Gas Mark 7).

6 Sprinkle with chopped parsley, and serve.

Burgundian meat balls

cooking time: about 30 minutes

you will need for 4 servings:

1 lb. raw minced beef	chopped parsley
2 oz. fresh white breadcrumbs	4 tablespoons oil
salt and pepper	1 packet oxtail soup
½ level teaspoon grated lemon rind	¾ pint water
1 small onion	¼ pint red wine
	4 oz. mushrooms, sliced

1 Mix meat, crumbs, seasoning, lemon rind, onion, and parsley.

2 Divide mixture into 8 portions and shape into balls.

3 Heat oil, add meat balls and brown. Remove from pan.

4 Blend soup into oil remaining in the pan. Stir in water and wine.

5 Bring to the boil, add mushrooms.

6 Reduce heat, replace meat balls. Cover and simmer for 20 minutes.

7 Serve with plain boiled spaghetti or noodles.

Chicken stew

cooking time: about 45 minutes

you will need for 4 servings:

1 packet chicken noodle soup	1 small red pepper (optional)
1¼ pints water	4 oz. peas
4 chicken joints	4 oz. French beans
8 oz. carrots	

1 Make up the soup as directed on the packet using 1¼ pints water.

2 Add the chicken joints. Chop the pepper if used, add to the soup, simmer for 30 minutes.

3 Add the vegetables and continue cooking until tender, about 15 minutes.

4 Serve with French bread.

Fricassée Suisse

cooking time: about 30 minutes

you will need for 4 servings:

packet asparagus soup	½ oz. cornflour
1¼ pints water	1 tablespoon milk
4 oz. chicken, cooked	1 egg yolk
4 oz. ham or bacon, cooked	¼ pint thin cream
	bacon rolls for garnishing

1 Make up soup using 1¼ pints water.

2 Cut chicken and ham into cubes, add to soup.

3 Blend cornflour to a smooth paste with milk.

4 Stir into soup and cook for 5 minutes, stirring throughout.

5 Mix egg yolk and cream together, beating lightly with a fork.

6 Stir a little of the hot soup into the egg mixture. Mix well. Pour back into the pan of soup.

7 Correct seasoning. Serve with bacon rolls.

Quick fricassée

cooking time: 10 minutes

you will need for 2 servings:

1 packet onion sauce	1 small can button mushrooms
½ pint milk	
8 oz. diced cooked lamb	

1 Make up the sauce as directed on the packet using ½ pint milk.

2 Stir in the lamb and mushrooms. Heat through.

3 Serve with rice or creamed potatoes.

Chilli hot pot

cooking time: about 30 minutes

you will need for 4 servings:

2 onions	1 packet tomato soup
1 clove garlic	¾ pint water
1 green pepper	1-lb. can red kidney beans
1 tablespoon oil	
1 lb. raw minced beef	1¼ level teaspoons chilli powder

1 Slice onions finely, chop garlic, cut pepper into thin strips.

2 Heat oil, sauté onions, garlic, pepper and beef until well browned.

3 Stir in tomato soup.

4 Gradually stir in water, bring to the boil.

5 Add the kidney beans and chilli powder.

6 Reduce heat, cover and simmer until meat is tender. Serve with French bread.

Farmhouse casserole

cooking time: about 30 minutes

you will need for 4 servings:

12 oz. cooked chicken
4 oz. cooked peas
4 cooked carrots
1 oz. cornflour
1 packet chicken
  vegetable soup
¾ pint water
1 11-oz. can creamed
  corn
1 teaspoon Worcester
  sauce
salt and pepper
2 oz. cheese, grated
2 oz. fresh white
  breadcrumbs

1 Slice chicken. Arrange with peas and carrots in layers in a casserole.
2 Mix cornflour with contents of packet of soup in a saucepan. Stir in corn, water and sauce.
3 Bring to the boil, stirring. Season to taste, pour into casserole.
4 Mix cheese and breadcrumbs together, sprinkle over the top of the casserole.
5 Bake in a moderately hot oven (375°F – Gas Mark 5) for 25 minutes.

Quick spaghetti bolognese

cooking time: 15 minutes

you will need for 4 servings:

1 lb. raw minced beef
1 packet oxtail soup
1 stick celery,
  chopped
½ green pepper,
  chopped
¾ pint water
4 mushrooms, sliced
8 oz. spaghetti
Parmesan cheese,
  grated

1 Put the minced beef, soup, celery and green pepper into a saucepan.
2 Stir in the water, bring to the boil. Reduce the heat and simmer for 10 minutes, stirring occasionally.
3 Add the mushrooms and cook for a further 5 minutes.
4 Meanwhile, cook spaghetti in boiling salted water until tender.
5 Drain spaghetti, pile in a hot dish, pour sauce over and sprinkle with Parmesan cheese.
6 Serve extra cheese separately.

Potato and leek fry

cooking time: 15–20 minutes

you will need for 4 servings:

1 lb. potatoes
2 leeks
2 oz. butter
salt and pepper
4 oz. cooked chopped
  meat
1 oz. grated cheese
little chopped parsley

1 Shred or grate the potatoes and chop the leeks finely.
2 Fry slowly in the butter until well browned on the under side. Turn over and continue the cooking until the potato is well cooked. Season carefully.
3 Add the meat and cheese and heat through.
4 Put on to a serving dish and sprinkle with chopped parsley.

Italian potato pie

cooking time: 20–25 minutes

you will need for 4 servings:

1 small onion, peeled
  and chopped
1 oz. butter
8 oz. cooked minced
  meat
1 14-oz. can tomatoes
2–3 olives, sliced
1 oz. seedless raisins
1 hard-boiled egg,
  sliced
salt and pepper
1 lb. mashed potato
little milk

1 Sauté the onion in the butter in a saucepan until soft.
2 Add the meat, olives, raisins and tomatoes.
3 Stir all together until quite hot. If the mixture is a little thin, add 1 level dessertspoon cornflour mixed smoothly with a little cold water. Bring to boiling point and boil for 1 minute.
4 Add hard-boiled egg and correct the seasoning.
5 Pour into a fireproof dish, cover with mashed potato and brush over with a little milk.
6 Bake for about 20 minutes in a moderately hot oven (375°F – Gas Mark 5).

Norfolk pork sausages

cooking time: about 30 minutes

you will need:

1 lb. sausages
1 small onion
¾ pint milk
salt and pepper
1 level tablespoon
  cornflour
1 level teaspoon dry
  mustard

1 Prick each sausage in several places with a fork.
2 Peel and finely chop the onion.
3 In a saucepan heat all but two tablespoons of the milk with the onion.
4 Drop in the sausages and simmer gently for about 20 minutes.
5 Lift out sausages and keep hot.
6 Blend the cornflour and mustard with the

remaining cold milk and pour the hot milk on to it, stirring continuously.

7 Return to the pan and stir until it boils, and boil gently for 5 minutes.
8 Season to taste.
9 Return the sausages to the pan and simmer for 5 minutes.

Sausage Palermo

cooking time: 20 minutes

you will need for 4 servings:

2 tablespoons corn oil	¾ pint water
1 onion, finely chopped	3 tablespoons white wine
1 lb. large pork sausages	2¼-oz. can tomato purée

1 chicken stock cube	6 oz. noodles
½ oz. cornflour	¼ oz. butter

1 Heat the corn oil and fry the onion and sausages until lightly browned.
2 Remove sausages from the pan and add the chicken stock cube and cornflour and cook for 1 minute.
3 Stir in the water, white wine and tomato purée and bring to the boil, stirring all the time.
4 Return the sausages to the sauce and simmer gently for 15 minutes.
5 Meanwhile cook the noodles in boiling salted water. Strain and toss in the butter.
6 Place in a flat casserole, arrange the sausages on top and pour the sauce over.

Egg and Cheese Dishes

There are probably no foods which lend themselves to a greater variety of occasions or recipes than eggs and cheese. Endlessly adaptable, simple to prepare, and consistently tasty and satisfying to eat, they remain among the housewife's most reliable allies. The following passages include a number of tempting new ways of dealing with these old favourites.

Basic recipe for a plain omelette

cooking time: 1–1½ minutes

you will need for 1 person:

2 eggs	salt and pepper
2 teaspoons water	½ oz. butter

1 Have ready the pan and the dish on which the omelette is to be served.
2 Break the eggs one at a time and put into a basin with the water and seasoning.
3 Heat the butter, pour in the egg mixture and as it sets, move the pan around and stir with a fork so that the still liquid mixture comes in contact with the hot pan.
4 When the egg is set to your taste, loosen the edges, tilt the pan away from you and with the help of a palette knife fold the omelette over.
5 Turn out on to a hot dish.

With herbs and ham: Chopped parsley, mixed herbs, a little finely chopped ham, etc., can be mixed with the eggs before frying. If a more substantial filling is used, put this on one half of the omelette before folding over.

With cheese: Sprinkle grated cheese over the centre of the omelette while cooking.

With onion: Mix 1 tablespoon chopped onion and 1 teaspoon chopped parsley. Add to omelette before cooking.

With vegetables: Use any left-over cooked vegetables. Force vegetables through a sieve, moisten with a little milk or gravy and season. Spread mixture lightly over omelette before folding.

Peasant style omelette

cooking time: 2–3 minutes

you will need for 4 servings:

2–3 small cold cooked potatoes	1 teaspoon chopped chives
1 oz. butter	salt and pepper
2–3 eggs	

1 Dice the potatoes and fry in the butter until well browned.
2 Beat the eggs lightly, add the chives and seasoning.
3 Add the potatoes to the eggs and then cook the omelette in the usual way.

Devilled omelette

cooking time: about 3 minutes

you will need for 4 servings:

3 eggs	2 tablespoons thin
salt, cayenne pepper	cream
¼ level teaspoon dry	2 oz. cooked ham,
mustard	chopped
pinch curry powder	½ oz. butter
2 tablespoons water	

1 Beat the eggs lightly and all the other ingredients except the butter.
2 Heat the butter in an omelette pan, add the egg mixture and cook fairly quickly, stirring occasionally and loosening the omelette from the side of the pan.
3 When lightly set on the under side, put the pan under the grill to brown the top.
4 Fold over and serve at once.

Spanish omelette

cooking time: 5 minutes to cook filling; 1½–2 minutes for the omelette

you will need for 4 servings:

For the filling:

1 small onion	1 tablespoon tarragon
2 tomatoes	vinegar
1 tablespoon oil	cayenne pepper

For the omelette:

3 eggs	
¾ oz. butter	3 teaspoons water

1 Peel and chop the onion very finely, peel and slice the tomatoes.
2 Heat the oil and cook the onion and tomato until the onion is tender, but not coloured.
3 Add vinegar and pepper.
4 Cook the omelette and put the filling in the centre before folding over.

Fish omelette

cooking time: 4–5 minutes

you will need for 4 servings:

3 eggs	lemon juice
1 teaspoon chopped	3 tablespoons cooked
parsley	fish
salt and pepper	1 oz. butter

1 Separate the eggs.
2 Beat the yolks and add parsley, seasoning and a squeeze of lemon juice.
3 Add the fish, flaked very finely.
4 Beat egg whites stiffly and fold into mixture.
5 Heat the butter in an omelette pan, pour in

the mixture and stir until it begins to set and is lightly browned on the under-side.
6 Put the pan under the grill to brown.

Chinese vegetable omelette

cooking time: 10–15 minutes

you will need for 4 servings:

1 medium-sized onion	1–2 sticks celery
1 oz. butter	½ green pepper
4 eggs	2 oz. mushrooms
salt and pepper	

1 Peel and chop the onion very finely and cook in the butter until soft and lightly browned.
2 Beat the eggs lightly and add the seasoning.
3 Chop the celery, green pepper and mushrooms very finely and add to the eggs.
4 Pour the egg mixture into the pan with the onion and stir until the eggs are firm.
5 Serve alone or with mushroom sauce, page 83.

Basque omelette

cooking time: 15–20 minutes

you will need for 4 servings:

2 green peppers	½ clove garlic
2 tablespoons oil	3 eggs
1 small onion	salt and pepper
3 tomatoes	slices buttered toast

1 Wash the peppers, remove the seeds and slice very thinly.
2 Heat the oil, add the peppers and the onion, chopped very finely and sauté all together.
3 When nearly cooked, add tomatoes, peeled and sliced and garlic, crushed.
4 Continue cooking until the peppers become quite soft and mushy.
5 Add the beaten eggs and stir briskly until they are cooked.
6 Season carefully and serve on toast.

Swiss omelette

cooking time: about 10 minutes

you will need for 4 servings:

1 oz. butter	2 tablespoons cooked
1 small onion, finely	green peas
chopped	2 oz. mushrooms,
1 cooked potato, cut	sliced
into dice	4 eggs
2 tomatoes, peeled	salt and pepper
and sliced	paprika

1 Melt the butter in a good sized frying pan or sauté pan.

2 Add the onion and cook until soft, then add potato, tomatoes, peas and mushrooms, and sauté all well together.
3 Beat the eggs, add a little seasoning and pour over the contents of the pan.
4 Cook until the egg is just set, then turn upside down on to a hot dish.
5 Sprinkle with paprika and garnish as liked.

Baked soufflé omelette

cooking time: 20–25 minutes

you will need for 4 servings:

1 oz. butter	⅛ teaspoon made
1 oz. cornflour	mustard
½ pint milk	4 eggs
salt and pepper	4 tomatoes
1 oz. grated cheese	

1 Make a sauce with the butter, cornflour and milk.
2 Add salt, pepper, grated cheese and mustard.
3 Add the egg yolks and fold in the stiffly beaten egg whites. Turn into a 5-in. soufflé dish or 1½ pint pie dish.
4 Bake until set and lightly browned – about 20 minutes in a moderately hot oven (375°F – Gas Mark 5).
5 While the omelette is cooking – bake the tomatoes cut in halves and use to garnish the dish.

Sweet corn soufflé

cooking time: 20 minutes

you will need for 4 servings:

1 can creamed sweet	salt and pepper
corn	2 eggs
1 oz. butter	

1 Put the sweet corn into a pan with the butter and seasoning and heat through.
2 Stir in the egg yolks one at a time.
3 Beat the egg whites stiffly and fold into the mixture.
4 Put into a fairly deep fireproof dish and bake about 20 minutes in a moderately hot oven (375°F – Gas Mark 5).

Welsh rarebit soufflé

cooking time: 4–5 minutes

you will need for 4 servings:

For the soufflé mixture:

½ oz. cornflour	2 eggs
¼ pint milk	½ oz. butter
salt and pepper	

For the filling:

1 oz. cheese, chopped	1 tablespoon milk
or grated	salt and pepper
½ oz. butter	a little made mustard

1 Mix the cornflour smoothly with the milk, put into a pan, bring to boiling point and boil for 1 minute stirring all the time.
2 Add seasoning and when cooled add yolks.
3 Beat whites stiffly and fold into mixture.
4 Heat the butter in an omelette pan, pour in the mixture and cook until lightly browned on the under side, then brown under the grill.
5 Melt the cheese with the butter, milk and seasoning. Pour over the omelette, fold in half and serve at once.

Savoury pancakes

cooking time: 4–5 minutes

you will need for 4 servings:

4 oz. plain flour	1 egg
pinch salt	½ pint milk

1 Sift the flour and salt into a bowl.
2 Make a well in the centre, add the egg and a little of the milk, beat, adding extra milk to make a smooth thick batter. Beat again for 2–3 minutes. Cover and leave to stand for as long as possible.
3 When required, add the rest of the milk.

To cook pancakes

1 Melt a little unsalted butter in a small frying pan. There should be enough fat only to give a thin film over the bottom of the pan.
2 Pour in enough batter to give a thin layer, tilting the pan so that the bottom is evenly covered.
3 Move the pan around while the pancake is cooking and loosen it from the sides of the pan.
4 When set and lighly browned on the under side, turn with a palette knife and brown the other side. Use as required. Pancakes will keep hot in the oven or over a pan of hot water if stacked with a piece of greaseproof paper between each one.

Chicken and mushroom pancakes

cooking time: 10 minutes for filling

you will need for 4 servings:

½ pint pancake batter	1 level tablespoon flour
1 oz. butter	¼ pint stock or milk
4 oz. chicken livers	2 oz. cooked chicken
2 oz. mushrooms	salt and pepper

1 Heat the butter.
2 Chop the livers and mushrooms and cook until the mushrooms are tender.
3 Stir in the flour and mix well.
4 Add stock, stir until boiling and boil for 1 minute.
5 Add chopped chicken and season carefully.
6 Make the pancakes (as before) and as each one is cooked, put a spoonful of the filling in the centre and roll up.
7 Put into a fireproof dish and keep hot.
8 If liked, serve with cheese or tomato sauce, see page 83.

Egg and cheese pancakes

cooking time: 10–15 minutes for filling

you will need for 4 servings:

2 hard-boiled eggs, sliced	½ pint pancake batter (see page 37)
8 oz. cooked chopped vegetables	½ pint cheese sauce (see page 83)
seasoning	

1 Mix the eggs and vegetables together and season carefully.
2 Make the pancakes (see page 37), put a little of the filling on each one and roll up.
3 When all are cooked, put into a fireproof dish, pour the sauce over and put into a moderately hot oven (375°F – Gas Mark 5), for about 10 minutes.

Florentine pancakes

cooking time: about 10 minutes for filling

you will need for 4 servings:

2 lb. spinach	½ pint pancake batter (see page 37)
salt and pepper	
nutmeg	8 oz. grated cheese
½ oz. butter	

1 Cook the spinach in the usual way, drain and chop very finely.
2 Add salt, pepper, nutmeg and butter.
3 Make the pancakes (see page 37) and pile on a hot dish, putting a layer of spinach and a generous sprinkling of cheese on each one.
4 Continue until the ingredients are used up, then top with grated cheese and serve cut into wedges.

Potato pancakes

cooking time: about 20 minutes

you will need for 4 servings:

4 oz. mashed potato	1 teaspoon onion juice
½ oz. butter	½ pint pancake batter (see page 37)
salt, pepper, nutmeg	
2 oz. finely chopped ham	½ pint cheese sauce (see page 83)
1 teaspoon chopped parsley	

1 Mix the potato with all the other ingredients (except the sauce) and beat well together.
2 Make the pancakes (see page 34), spread with the filling and roll up.
3 Put into a fireproof dish, coat with the sauce and heat through in the oven or under the grill.

Toasted cheese special

cooking time: 10 minutes

you will need for 4 servings:

4 slices bread	1 packet onion sauce mix
4 oz. Cheddar cheese, cut in four slices	½ pint milk
4 eggs	black pepper
1–2 tablespoons melted butter	

1 Toast the bread on one side.
2 Place a slice of cheese on each untoasted side of bread. Grill until the cheese has melted.
3 Meanwhile, fry the eggs in the butter.
4 Make up the onion sauce mix as directed on the packet using ½ pint milk. Place a fried egg on each slice of toast and pour the sauce over. Sprinkle with ground black pepper and serve.

Welsh rarebit

cooking time: 4–5 minutes

you will need for 4 servings:

1 oz. butter	1 tablespoon Worcester sauce or beer (optional)
1 oz. flour	
¼ pint milk	
1 level teaspoon made mustard	4 rounds of buttered toast
salt and pepper	
8 oz. grated cheese	

1 Heat the butter, add the flour and mix well.
2 Add the milk, stir until boiling and boil for 1 minute.

3 Add all the other ingredients, reserving a little of the cheese.

4 Heat gently until the cheese has melted, then spread on the toast.

5 Sprinkle with the remaining cheese and brown under the grill.

Spanish open sandwich

cooking time: 15 minutes

you will need for 4 servings:

1 tablespoon corn oil	½ pint milk
1 small onion, finely chopped	2 eggs
	salt and pepper
½ green pepper, finely chopped	2 oz. ham, chopped
	4 slices buttered toast
1 packet cheese sauce	

To garnish:
spring onions or
  slices of Spanish
  onion

1 Heat the corn oil and sauté the onion and pepper until tender.

2 Stir in the contents of the packet of cheese sauce, milk and the lightly beaten eggs.

3 Heat gradually until the mixture thickens, stirring all the time. Season to taste.

4 Add the ham.

5 Pile on to the buttered toast and garnish with spring onions or slices of Spanish onion.

Cheese and shrimp pie

cooking time: 10 minutes

you will need for 4 servings:

6 eggs	1 oz. butter
½ pint cheese sauce (see page 83)	1 oz. grated cheese
	2 tablespoons breadcrumbs
1 4-oz. can shrimps	

1 Boil the eggs for 7 minutes, then put into cold water for 1 minute before removing the shells.

2 Chop the eggs roughly, and mix with the sauce.

3 Add the shrimps and butter and correct the seasoning.

4 Pour into a greased fireproof dish. Sprinkle with the cheese and breadcrumbs mixed together and brown in a hot oven or under the grill.

Cheese eggs

cooking time: 2–3 minutes to fry

you will need for 4 servings:

6 oz. grated cheese	1 raw egg
1½ oz. plain flour	little milk
salt, cayenne pepper	4 hard-boiled eggs
few drops Worcester sauce	breadcrumbs

1 Mix the cheese, flour, seasonings and Worcester sauce together.

2 Bind with beaten egg and a little milk.

3 Coat the hard-boiled eggs with this mixture. Using wet hands will help.

4 Roll in breadcrumbs and fry in hot fat until golden brown.

5 Drain and serve hot with vegetables or serve cold with salad.

Cheese soufflé

cooking time: 25–30 minutes

you will need for 4 servings:

1 oz. butter	3 eggs
½ oz. cornflour	4 oz. grated cheese
¼ level teaspoon dry mustard	salt and pepper
	nutmeg
¼ pint milk	

1 Prepare a 6-in. soufflé dish or pie dish by greasing lightly.

2 Melt the butter, add the cornflour and mix well, stir in the mustard.

3 Add the milk gradually, stir until boiling and boil for 3 minutes.

4 Add egg yolks, cheese and seasoning.

5 Fold in the stiffly beaten egg whites.

6 Turn into the prepared dish and bake in a moderately hot oven (375°F – Gas Mark 5), until firm and set.

Easy cheese soufflé

cooking time: 30 minutes

you will need for 2 servings:

1 packet cheese sauce	2 eggs
¼ pint milk	

1 Grease a 5-in. soufflé dish.

2 Make up the cheese sauce as directed on the packet, using only ¼ pint milk.

3 Separate the eggs. Stir the yolks into the sauce.

4 Whisk whites until stiff and fold into sauce.

5 Pour into the soufflé dish. Bake in a moderately hot oven (375°F Gas Mark 5). Serve.

Cheese and raisin pie

cooking time: 30 minutes

you will need for 4 servings:

For cheese pastry:

6 oz. plain flour	1½ oz. lard
pinch salt	3 oz. grated cheese
1½ oz. butter	cold water to mix

For filling:

1 oz. butter	1 egg
1 oz. flour	4 oz. raisins
½ pint milk	4½ oz. grated cheese
salt and pepper	

1 Sift the flour and salt together. Rub in the fat.
2 Add grated cheese.
3 Add enough water to make a fairly firm dough.
4 Knead lightly, divide in half and use half to line a fairly deep pie plate.
5 Make a sauce with the butter, flour and milk.
6 Season and add the lightly beaten egg, raisins and 4 oz. of the cheese.
7 Pour into the pastry-lined plate. Moisten the edges of the pastry and cover with the remaining pastry.
8 Press the edges well together and decorate as liked. Make an incision in the top of the pastry to allow the steam to escape.
9 Brush over with milk, sprinkle with rest of cheese and bake for about 30 minutes in a moderately hot oven (375°F – Gas Mark 5).

Cheese flan

cooking time: 20 minutes

you will need for 4 servings:

For flan case:

4 oz. plain flour	1 oz. lard
pinch salt	2 oz. grated cheese
1 oz. butter	cold water

For filling:

2 cooked carrots, sliced	2 tomatoes, peeled and sliced
2 tablespoons cooked peas	½ pint cheese sauce (see page 83)
2 hard-boiled eggs, sliced	½ oz. grated cheese

1 Make the pastry as described in the recipe for cheese and raisin pie (see above).
2 Roll out and line a flan ring or sandwich tin.
3 Prick the bottom, put in a piece of greaseproof paper and half fill with baking beans or crusts of bread.
4 Bake for about 20 minutes in a moderately hot oven (375°F – Gas Mark 5).
5 Remove the beans just before the pastry is cooked.
6 Arrange the vegetables and eggs in the cooked flan case alternately with the sauce in layers, finishing with sauce.
7 Sprinkle with grated cheese and brown under the grill or heat through in the oven.

Cheese pudding

cooking time: 25–30 minutes

you will need for 4 servings:

6–8 slices bread and butter	2 teaspoons Worcester sauce
2 eggs	4 oz. grated cheese
salt and pepper	1 pint milk
¼ level teaspoon made mustard	1 tablespoon breadcrumbs
1 small onion, finely chopped	

1 Put the slices of bread and butter into a greased fireproof dish.
2 Beat up the eggs with the seasonings and add the onion, Worcester sauce and most of the cheese.
3 Stir in the milk, then pour into the pie dish and leave to stand for about 10 minutes.
4 Mix the remaining cheese and breadcrumbs together, sprinkle on top of the pudding and bake in a moderate oven (350°F – Gas Mark 4) until the pudding is set.

Cheese and onion pudding

cooking time: about 20 minutes

you will need for 4 servings:

8 oz. onions	4 oz. grated cheese
1 pint milk	salt and pepper
6 oz. fresh breadcrumbs	cayenne pepper
3 eggs	chopped parsley

1 Peel and slice the onions thinly and cook slowly in the milk until just tender.
2 Remove from the heat, add the breadcrumbs and beaten eggs and most of the cheese.
3 Season very carefully with salt, pepper and a little cayenne pepper.
4 Turn into a greased fireproof dish, sprinkle with the remaining cheese and bake about 20 minutes in a moderate oven (350°F – Gas Mark 4). Sprinkle with chopped parsley.

Cheese crisp

cooking time: about 15 minutes

you will need for 4 servings:

1 oz. butter
1 oz. flour
¾ pint stock or milk
4 oz. grated cheese
salt and pepper
2 hard-boiled eggs
4 oz. cooked mixed
vegetables

4 oz. cooked diced
meat
little chopped red
pepper
2 packets potato
crisps

1 Make a sauce with the butter, flour and stock or milk.
2 Add most of the cheese and season carefully.
3 Pour a little of the sauce into a fireproof dish, slice the eggs and arrange on top.
4 Add the vegetables, meat and pepper to the remaining sauce and heat through.
5 Pour into the dish.
6 Crush the potato crisps, mix with the remaining cheese and sprinkle on top.
7 Put under the grill to brown.

Cheese pie

cooking time: 20–25 minutes

you will need for 4 servings:

3 oz. breadcrumbs
½ pint boiling milk
3 oz. grated cheese
1 oz. butter

1 egg
salt and pepper
nutmeg

1 Put the breadcrumbs into a basin and pour on the boiling milk. Leave to stand for 10 minutes.
2 Add cheese, butter, egg yolk and seasonings.
3 Beat the egg white stiffly and fold into the mixture.
4 Pour into a greased fireproof dish and bake in a moderately hot oven (375°F – Gas Mark 5), until set.

Cheese and potato pie

cooking time: 20–25 minutes

you will need for 4 servings:

1½ lb. cooked potatoes
1 oz. butter
little milk

salt and pepper
nutmeg

For filling:

1 oz. butter
1 oz. cornflour
½ pint milk
4 oz. grated cheese

2 oz. breadcrumbs
2 eggs
salt and pepper

1 Mash the potatoes with the butter and a little milk and season well.
2 Use to line a greased pie dish, having a thin layer of the potato over the bottom of the dish.
3 Make a sauce with the butter, cornflour and milk and add cheese, breadcrumbs, egg yolks and seasoning.
4 Beat the egg whites stiffly and fold into the mixture.
5 Turn into the prepared dish and bake about 20 minutes in a moderately hot oven (375°F – Gas Mark 5).

Swiss cheese tart

cooking time: 25 minutes

you will need for 4 servings:

4 oz. rough puff
pastry or flaky pastry
(see page 86)
2 eggs
½ oz. butter

¼ pint thin cream or
evaporated milk
4 oz. grated cheese
salt and pepper

1 Roll the pastry thinly and use it to line a shallow fireproof dish. Decorate the edge as liked.
2 Beat the eggs, add the butter, cream, cheese and seasoning.
3 Pour into pastry case and bake in a moderately hot oven (375°F – Gas Mark 5).

Corn cheese bake

cooking time: 20 minutes

you will need for 4 servings:

1 packet cheese sauce
½ pint milk
4-oz. can prawns
16-oz. can cream
style corn
2 sticks celery,
chopped

3 spring onions,
chopped
salt and pepper
8 oz. Patna rice

1 Make up the cheese sauce as directed on the packet, using ½ pint milk.
2 Stir most of the prawns into the sauce, reserving a few for garnish.
3 Add corn, celery, onions and seasoning to taste. Heat through slowly for 10–15 minutes.
4 Cook the rice in boiling salted water until tender. Drain well.
5 Arrange the rice round the edge of a serving dish. Pour the sauce into the centre and garnish with remaining prawns.

Egg and cheese cutlets

cooking time: 4–5 minutes to fry

you will need for 4 servings:

2 oz. butter	cayenne pepper
2 oz. flour	4 hard-boiled eggs
½ pint milk	2 oz. grated cheese
salt and pepper	egg and breadcrumbs

1 Make a thick sauce with the butter, flour and milk.
2 Season carefully with salt, pepper and cayenne.
3 Add the eggs chopped finely and the cheese. Mix well.
4 Spread the mixture on to a wetted plate and leave to cool.
5 Divide into equal portions and shape each into a cutlet shape.
6 Coat with egg and breadcrumbs and fry in deep fat.

Note: A piece of macaroni can be inserted in the narrow end of the cutlet, if liked.

Eggs bonne femme

cooking time: 20 minutes

you will need for 4 servings:

8 oz. onions	salt and pepper
2 oz. butter	nutmeg
1 dessertspoon white vinegar	3 oz. breadcrumbs
4 eggs	4 oz. grated Parmesan cheese

1 Peel and slice the onions thinly and cook in 1 oz. of the butter until soft.
2 Add the vinegar and mix well.
3 Put the onions into a greased fireproof dish and break the eggs on top. Season carefully.
4 Heat the remaining 1 oz. butter, add the breadcrumbs and cook until pale brown.
5 Stir in the cheese and sprinkle the crumbs over the eggs.
6 Bake in a moderate oven (350°F – Gas Mark 4), until set.

Egg and ham flan

cooking time: 15 minutes

you will need for 4 servings:

6 eggs	¼ pint white sauce (see page 82)
½ oz. butter	
1 level teaspoon made mustard	1 7-in. baked pastry case
4 oz. chopped cooked ham	grated cheese

1 Boil the eggs for 7 minutes, then remove shells and cut into slices.
2 Melt the butter in a pan, add the mustard and ham and sauté for a few minutes.
3 Add the sauce and eggs. Season carefully.
4 Pour into the pastry case, sprinkle with grated cheese and brown under the grill.

Egg and mushroom savoury

cooking time: about 15 minutes

you will need for 4 servings:

4 eggs	½ pint milk
2 oz. butter	salt and pepper
4 oz. mushrooms, chopped	parsley and paprika to garnish
1 oz. cornflour	fingers of toast

1 Boil the eggs for 7 minutes, put into cold water for 1 minute and remove the shells.
2 Melt the butter, add the mushrooms and cook until just tender – about 5 minutes.
3 Stir in the cornflour and mix well.
4 Add the milk, stir until boiling and boil for 3 minutes, season carefully.
5 Cut the eggs in halves and put into a serving dish.
6 Pour the sauce over and garnish with chopped parsley and paprika. Serve with fingers of toast.

Curried eggs

cooking time: 25–30 minutes

you will need for 4 servings:

4–6 hard-boiled eggs	2 teaspoons cornflour
1 small onion, peeled and chopped	½ pint stock or water salt
1 small apple, peeled and chopped	lemon juice
2 oz. butter	4 oz. Patna rice, cooked for 12 minutes in boiling salted water
2 teaspoons curry powder	
½ level teaspoon curry paste	

1 Shell the eggs and cut into halves.
2 Fry the onion and apple in the butter for a few minutes, then add curry powder, curry paste and cornflour and mix well. Continue cooking for a further 3–4 minutes.
3 Add the stock, stir until boiling.
4 Add seasoning and lemon juice. Cover and simmer for about 20 minutes.

5 Put the eggs into the sauce to heat through, then place on top of rice and pour the sauce over.

Macaroni and egg savoury

cooking time: 15 minutes

you will need for 4 servings:

3 oz. macaroni	1 oz. butter
½ pint milk	1 oz. flour
¼ pint water in which macaroni was cooked	4 oz. grated cheese salt and pepper 4 eggs

1 Break up the macaroni and cook in boiling salted water for about 15 minutes until tender.
2 Strain and reserve ¼ pint of the water.
3 Use this with the milk and make a sauce with the butter and flour.
4 Add most of the grated cheese and seasoning.
5 Put into a shallow fireproof dish.
6 Make four hollows and drop in the eggs.
7 Sprinkle with the remaining cheese and a little salt and pepper and bake in a moderately hot oven (375°F – Gas Mark 5).

Stuffed tomatoes

cooking time: 15 minutes

you will need for 3–4 servings:

6–8 large firm tomatoes	4 oz. grated cheese 1 egg
3 tablespoons breadcrumbs	salt cayenne pepper
pinch mixed herbs	4 oz. spaghetti

1 Cut a slice from the stalk end of each tomato and scoop out the centre being careful not to break the tomato skin.
2 Mix the breadcrumbs, herbs and most of the cheese. Bind with the beaten egg and season carefully.
3 Fill the tomatoes with this mixture and bake about 15 minutes in a moderate oven (375°F. – Gas Mark 4).
4 Break up the spaghetti and cook in boiling salted water. Drain.
5 Add the remaining cheese and pulp from the tomatoes. Reheat and add seasoning if required.
6 Pour the spaghetti into a hot dish and arrange the tomatoes on top.

Eggs boulangère

cooking time: 15–20 minutes

you will need for 4 servings:

3–4 cold cooked potatoes	3 oz. grated cheese 4 eggs
1 oz. butter	2 tablespoons thin cream or top of milk
salt and pepper nutmeg	

1 Slice the potatoes and fry in the butter until brown on both sides.
2 Put into a greased fireproof dish and season with salt, pepper and a pinch of nutmeg.
3 Sprinkle the cheese on top.
4 Break each egg carefully on top of the cheese, sprinkle with salt and pepper and cover with the cream or milk.
5 Bake about 10 minutes in a moderate oven (350°F – Gas Mark 4).

Eggs au gratin on spinach

cooking time: 10–15 minutes

you will need for 4 servings:

1½ lb. fresh spinach or large packet frozen spinach	nutmeg 4 eggs ½ pint cheese sauce (see page 83)
1 oz. butter	
salt and pepper	little grated cheese

1 Cook the spinach, drain well and chop up with the butter. Add seasoning and a pinch of nutmeg.
2 Put the spinach into a fireproof dish.
3 Poach the eggs and arrange on top.
4 Cover with cheese sauce, sprinkle with grated cheese and brown under the grill.

Savoury eggs No. 1

cooking time: 10–15 minutes

you will need for 4 servings:

6 hard-boiled eggs	little oil or melted butter
2–3 oz. cold cooked fish	salt and pepper
1 teaspoon capers, chopped	½ pint cheese sauce (see page 83)

1 Cut eggs in half lengthways and remove the yolks.
2 Put the yolks into a basin with the fish, capers and enough oil to make a smooth paste.
3 Season carefully and fill the egg whites with this mixture.
4 Put into a fireproof dish, pour the sauce over and brown under the grill.

Savoury eggs No. 2

cooking time: 20 minutes

you will need for 4 servings:

2 tablespoons corn oil	½ pint milk
4 oz. mushrooms, sliced	1 oz. cheese, grated
4 eggs, hard-boiled	1 oz. white breadcrumbs
1 packet white sauce	

To garnish: bacon rolls

1 Heat the corn oil and sauté the mushrooms until tender. Put into a fireproof dish.
2 Slice eggs and place on top of mushrooms.
3 Make up the white sauce as directed on the packet using ½ pint milk. Pour the sauce over the ingredients in the dish.
4 Mix together the cheese and breadcrumbs and sprinkle over the top.
5 Bake in a moderate oven (350°F – Gas Mark 4) for 10–15 minutes. Place under a hot grill to brown the top.
6 Garnish with bacon rolls and serve.

Egg and cheese fricassée

cooking time: 15–20 minutes

you will need for 4 servings:

4 hard-boiled eggs	salt and pepper
½ pint white sauce (see page 82)	6 oz. grated cheese
1 tablespoon chopped parsley	1 tablespoon breadcrumbs
¼ level teaspoon grated nutmeg	

1 Slice the eggs and put into a fireproof dish.
2 Make the white sauce.
3 Add parsley, nutmeg, seasoning and about 4 oz. of the cheese.
4 Pour over the eggs.
5 Mix the rest of the cheese and the breadcrumbs together and sprinkle over the top.
6 Brown in a moderately hot oven (375°F – Gas Mark 5) or under the grill.

Celery and cheese au gratin

cooking time: about 15 minutes

you will need for 4 servings:

1 large can celery hearts (or 1–2 heads fresh celery, if time permits)	½ pint white sauce – using ¼ pint milk and ¼ pint liquid from the celery
1 oz. butter	2–3 tomatoes, peeled and sliced
3 oz. grated cheese	
squeeze lemon juice	

1 Drain the celery and put into a fireproof dish.
2 Make the white sauce, add butter, most of the cheese and the lemon juice. Pour over the celery.
3 Sprinkle the rest of the cheese on top and arrange slices of tomato round the edge.
4 Put into a hot oven (425°F – Gas Mark 7) for about 15 minutes to heat through.

Egg and shrimp savoury

cooking time: about 20 minutes

you will need for 4 servings:

4 eggs, boiled for 6 minutes	1 4-oz. can shrimps
1 oz. butter	1 small can evaporated milk
1 tablespoon chopped parsley	seasoning
1 teaspoon chopped chervil, if available	1 tablespoon grated cheese
¼ level teaspoon French mustard	

1 Peel and cut the eggs into slices.
2 Mix all the ingredients together, except the cheese, and season carefully.
3 Put into a greased fireproof dish, sprinkle with cheese and brown in a moderately hot oven (375°F – Gas Mark 5).

Savoury custard tart

cooking time: 25–30 minutes

you will need for 4 servings:

1 7-in. baked pastry case (see page 87)	3 eggs
2 oz. rashers bacon	1 oz. grated cheese
½ oz. butter	salt and pepper
½ small onion, finely chopped	cayenne pepper
	4 tablespoons milk

1 Remove the rind from the bacon, cut into pieces and fry in the butter with the onion.
2 When the onion is just tender, mix with the egg yolks and cheese, add seasoning and milk.
3 Beat whites stiffly and fold into egg mixture.
4 Pour into the pastry case and bake in a moderate oven (350°F – Gas Mark 4) until the mixture is firm and lightly browned.

Eggs Lorraine

cooking time: 10 minutes

you will need for 4 servings:

4–6 rashers of bacon	1 oz. butter
4 oz. cheese, grated coarsely	4 eggs
¼ pint thin cream or evaporated milk	seasoning
	a little chopped parsley

1 Trim the bacon and put into a shallow fireproof dish.
2 Cover with the grated cheese and pour over the cream.
3 Dot with butter.
4 Break each egg carefully on top, sprinkle with salt and pepper and put into a moderate oven (350°F – Gas Mark 4), until the eggs are set.
5 Sprinkle with parsley before serving.

Potato eggs

cooking time: 3–4 minutes to fry

you will need for 4 servings:

8 oz. cooked potatoes	¼ level teaspoon
1 egg yolk	grated nutmeg
½ oz. butter	1 oz. grated cheese
1 teaspoon chopped	4 hard-boiled eggs
parsley	egg and breadcrumbs
½ level teaspoon salt	fat for deep frying

1 Mix the potatoes with the egg yolk and butter and add parsley, salt, nutmeg and cheese.
2 Divide into four portions and coat the hard-boiled eggs.
3 Roll in flour, then coat with egg and breadcrumbs.
4 Fry in deep fat until crisp and golden.
5 Serve hot with salad.

Eggs Neapolitan

cooking time: about 20 minutes

you will need for 4 servings:

6 oz. rice	1 oz. butter
1 small onion, finely	2 tomatoes, peeled
chopped	and sliced
¼ pint tomato purée	4 hard-boiled eggs
(1 small can)	salt and pepper
¼ pint stock or water	little chopped parsley
3 oz. macaroni	

1 Wash the rice and put into a pan with the onion, tomato purée and stock.
2 Cook until the rice is tender.
3 Meanwhile, break up the macaroni and cook in boiling salted water.
4 Strain, add the butter and tomatoes.
5 Make a ring of the rice on a serving dish.
6 Cut the eggs in half and put in the centre and cover with macaroni.
7 Sprinkle with parsley before serving.

Quick egg rissoles

cooking time: 5–7 minutes

you will need for 4 servings:

4 hard-boiled eggs	salt and pepper
1 tablespoon flour	1 fresh egg
1 tablespoon finely	1–2 tablespoons thin
chopped parsley	cream or milk
2 tablespoons finely	breadcrumbs
chopped ham	fat for frying

1 Chop the hard-boiled eggs and mix with the flour, parsley, ham and seasoning.
2 Bind with the egg and cream.
3 Shape into rissoles, dip in milk and coat with breadcrumbs.
4 Fry in shallow fat until crisp and golden, turning once.

Egg à la tripe

cooking time: about 10 minutes

you will need for 4 servings:

6 hard-boiled eggs	½ pint basic white
3–4 medium-sized	sauce (see page 82)
onions	salt and pepper
2 oz. butter	chopped parsley

1 Cut the eggs into slices.
2 Peel and slice onions and sauté in the butter until soft and lightly coloured.
3 Make the white sauce, add salt and pepper.
4 Add the eggs and onions.
5 Pour into a serving dish and serve hot sprinkled with chopped parsley or a little red pepper.

Egg and mushroom au gratin

cooking time: about 10 minutes

you will need for 4 servings:

8 eggs	lemon juice
2 oz. butter	1 egg
8 oz. mushrooms	1 tablespoon thin
¼ pint basic white	cream
sauce (see page 82)	4 tablespoons grated
salt and pepper	Parmesan cheese

1 Boil the eggs for 6 minutes only.
2 Shell the eggs and chop coarsely.
3 Heat the butter and cook the sliced mushrooms in it, until just tender.
4 Make the white sauce, add salt and pepper and lemon juice. Cool a little.
5 Mix egg with cream and stir into sauce.
6 Add the eggs and the mushrooms.
7 Pour into a fireproof dish, sprinkle thickly with the cheese and heat through in a moderate oven (350°F – Gas Mark 4).

German cheese tart

cooking time: 30 minutes

you will need for 4 servings:

2 oz. cornflour
½ pint milk
2 eggs
3 oz. grated cheese

2 oz. currants and
sultanas, mixed
salt and pepper
1 7-in. baked pastry
case (see page 87)

1 Mix the cornflour smoothly with a little of the milk, then stir in the rest of the milk.
2 Add the beaten eggs, cheese and fruit.
3 Pour into the pastry case and bake for about 25–30 minutes in a moderately hot oven (370°F – Gas Mark 5).

Vegetable Dishes

Vegetables are too often relegated to the role of 'supporting cast' when, in fact, they can hold the centre of the stage themselves. Their success does of course depend on the imagination with which they are prepared and combined. And even if they are only used as accessories, the care with which they are cooked and served can greatly enhance the dish they accompany.

I think you will find both these facts borne out by the recipes which follow.

Quick mushroom risotto

cooking time: 15–20 minutes

you will need for 4 servings:

6 oz. rice
1 lb. mushrooms
2 oz. butter
salt and pepper

8 oz. cooked ham or
other cooked meat
1 tablespoon chopped
parsley

1 Cook the rice in boiling salted water for 12 minutes.
2 Meanwhile, chop the mushrooms and sauté in the butter for a few minutes.
3 Add the diced ham and cook all together until the mushrooms are tender.
4 Season and add parsley.
5 Drain the rice and rinse under hot water and put into a hot serving dish.
6 Pour the mushroom mixture on top.

Scalloped mushrooms

cooking time: about 20 minutes

you will need for 4 servings:

1 oz. butter
1 oz. cornflour
¾ pint milk
salt and pepper
nutmeg

8 oz. mushrooms
4 hard-boiled eggs
2 tomatoes
breadcrumbs
chopped parsley

1 Make a sauce with the butter, cornflour and milk and season with salt and pepper and a pinch of nutmeg.
2 Add the thinly sliced mushrooms and simmer for about 10 minutes.
3 Put the sliced hard-boiled eggs and peeled and sliced tomatoes into a fireproof dish.
4 Pour the mushrooms and sauce over.
5 Sprinkle with breadcrumbs and put into a moderately hot oven (375°F – Gas Mark 5) until brown and crisp.
6 Sprinkle with parsley before serving.

Mushroom rarebit

cooking time: about 20 minutes

you will need for 4 servings:

1 lb. mushrooms,
sliced
2 oz. butter
salt and pepper
1 tablespoon tomato
paste

2 tablespoons stock or
water
2 tablespoons grated
Parmesan cheese
4 slices buttered toast

1 Sauté the mushrooms in the butter slowly for about 10 minutes.
2 Add salt and pepper and the tomato paste mixed with the stock.
3 Add the cheese and continue slow cooking for a further 10 minutes.
4 Serve on hot buttered toast.

Glazed mushrooms with ham

cooking time: 10–15 minutes

you will need for 4 servings:

2 oz. butter
2 tablespoons brown
sugar
1 teaspoon plain flour
1 lb. mushrooms,
thickly sliced

¼ level teaspoon
grated nutmeg
¼ level teaspoon
powdered mace
4–6 slices cooked ham
3 tablespoons sherry

1 Melt the butter, add the sugar and flour mixed together and heat slowly until the sugar has melted.
2 Add mushrooms, nutmeg and mace. Cover and cook very slowly for 5 minutes.
3 Remove the cover, put the ham over the mushrooms and increase the heat so that the ham is heated through.
4 Add the sherry, then turn out upside-down on to a serving dish.

Onion crisp

cooking time: about 25 minutes

you will need for 4 servings:

1 lb. small onions	salt and pepper
½ pint milk	1–2 packets potato
4 oz. cooked green	crisps
peas	2 tablespoons finely
2½ oz. butter	chopped or minced
2 oz. flour	nuts

1 Peel the onions, cut in halves, unless very small, and cook in the milk with a little water until tender.
2 Drain and put into a greased fireproof dish with the peas. Reserve the liquid.
3 Melt 2 oz. of the butter, add the flour and mix well.
4 Add ½ pint of the liquid in which the onions were cooked, stir until boiling and boil for 1 minute. Season carefully.
5 Pour the sauce over the onions and peas.
6 Crumble the potato crisps, mix with the nuts and sprinkle on top of the sauce. Add butter.
7 Brown the top under the grill or in a hot oven.

Baked stuffed onions

cooking time: 30 minutes

you will need for 4 servings:

4 medium-sized	salt and pepper
onions	butter
2 tablespoons	½ pint white sauce
breadcrumbs	(see page 82)
3 oz. grated cheese	mashed potatoes

1 Peel the onions and parboil in boiling salted water.
2 Drain and cool a little, then remove some of the inside with a small teaspoon.
3 Chop the onion which has been removed and mix with the breadcrumbs and half the cheese. Season carefully.

4 Add a little of the white sauce to moisten if necessary.
5 Fill the onions with this mixture, sprinkle with the rest of the cheese and dot with butter.
6 Bake in a moderately hot oven (375°F – Gas Mark 5).
7 Serve on a bed of hot mashed potato and serve the sauce separately.

Scalloped onions

cooking time: 20 minutes

you will need for 4 servings:

1½ lb. onions	cayenne pepper
1 oz. butter	4 oz. cooked ham
1 oz. flour	2 oz. grated Parmesan
½ pint milk	or Gruyère cheese
salt and pepper	

1 Peel the onions, cut into thick slices and cook in boiling salted water until tender.
2 Drain and put half into a greased fireproof dish.
3 Make a sauce with the butter, flour and milk. Season well.
4 Pour some of the sauce over the onions.
5 Cover with the chopped ham and the rest of the onions and the remaining sauce.
6 Sprinkle with cheese and bake in a hot oven (425°F – Gas Mark 7).

Mushroom and fish pie

cooking time: 20 minutes

you will need for 4 servings:

2 onions, peeled and	salt and pepper
finely chopped	lemon juice
2 oz. butter	1 lb. cooked, mashed
4–6 oz. mushrooms	potato
1 lb. fillets of white	little milk
fish	chopped parsley

1 Fry the onion in the butter until soft.
2 Add the chopped mushrooms and cook over a gentle heat for about 5 minutes. Season.
3 Put half the fish into a greased fireproof dish, add half the mushroom mixture, then the rest of the fish and the rest of the mushrooms.
4 Cover with the potato, brush over with a little milk and dot with butter.
5 Bake in a moderately hot oven (375°F – Gas Mark 5).
6 Sprinkle with parsley before serving.

Aubergines à la Provence

cooking time: 20–30 minutes

you will need for 4 servings:

2 aubergines	½ small onion, finely
8 oz. tomatoes,	chopped
peeled and	2 tablespoons
sliced	breadcrumbs
1 oz. butter	seasoning

1 Wipe the aubergines. Cut in half lengthways and remove the pulp (do not peel).
2 Sprinkle a little salt into the aubergine cases. Turn upside down and leave for 30 minutes. This is to remove excess water.
3 Fry the tomatoes in the butter with the onion and pulp from the aubergines.
4 Add the breadcrumbs and season with salt and pepper.
5 Drain and wipe the aubergine shells and pile in the filling.
6 Sprinkle a few more breadcrumbs over the filling and bake in a moderate oven (350°F – Gas Mark 4).

Aubergines with meat filling

cooking time: 25–30 minutes

you will need for 4 servings:

2 aubergines	1 oz. mushrooms,
2 tablespoons chopped	chopped
cooked meat	salt and pepper
1 tablespoon finely	1 egg
chopped onion	breadcrumbs
1 teaspoon chopped	½ oz. butter
parsley	

1 Prepare the aubergines as described in the recipe for Aubergines à la Provence, above.
2 Mix the pulp with the meat, onion, parsley and mushrooms, and season well.
3 Bind with beaten egg and pile into the aubergine shells.
4 Sprinkle with breadcrumbs, dot with butter and bake at 350°F – Gas Mark 4.

Aubergines with rice and cheese

cooking time: 25 minutes

you will need for 4 servings:

2 aubergines	2 oz. grated cheese
1 shallot, finely	2 oz. cooked rice
chopped	salt and pepper
½ small clove garlic	

1 Prepare the aubergines as described in the recipe for Aubergines à la Provence.
2 Put the pulp into a basin with the shallot, garlic, most of the cheese, rice, salt and pepper. Mix all well together.
3 Pile into the aubergine shells, sprinkle with the remaining cheese and bake in a moderate oven (350°F – Gas Mark 4).

Beans au gratin

cooking time: about 20 minutes

you will need for 4 servings:

1½ lb. scarlet runner	½ pint chicken or other
or French beans	white stock
2 small onions	nutmeg
1 oz. butter	4 oz. grated cheese
1 oz. flour	1 tablespoon chopped
salt and pepper	parsley

1 Prepare and slice the beans. Cook in boiling salted water until tender.
2 Meanwhile, peel and slice the onions thinly and fry in the butter until golden brown.
3 Add the flour and mix well.
4 Add the stock gradually. Stir until boiling and stir for 1 minute. Add seasoning and a good pinch of nutmeg.
5 When the beans are tender, drain thoroughly and add them to the sauce.
6 Add most of the cheese and turn into a serving dish.
7 Sprinkle the remaining cheese and parsley on top.

Broad beans with rice

cooking time: about 10 minutes

you will need for 4 servings:

3–4 rashers streaky	4 oz. cooked rice
bacon	½ oz. butter
¼ pint yoghourt	1 egg yolk
salt and pepper	
8 oz. cooked broad	
beans	

1 Chop the bacon into small pieces and fry until crisp.
2 Add to the yoghourt with a little seasoning.
3 Add the beans, rice and butter and stir over a gentle heat until the mixture is well heated through.
4 Stir in the egg yolk and reheat without boiling.

Chicory and ham au gratin

cooking time: about 30 minutes

you will need for 4 servings:

4 heads of chicory	2 oz. grated cheese
lemon juice	1 tablespoon thin
4 slices of cooked	cream
ham	½ oz. butter
½ pint basic white	
sauce (see page 82)	

1 Parboil the chicory in boiling water to which a squeeze of lemon juice has been added.
2 Drain, then wrap each in a slice of ham and put into a fireproof dish.
3 Make up the white sauce, add half the cheese, cream and lemon juice to taste.
4 Pour over the chicory, sprinkle the rest of the cheese on top and dot with butter.
5 Put into a moderate oven (350°F – Gas Mark 4), until the sauce begins to colour and the chicory is tender.

Cauliflower and egg savoury

cooking time: about 20 minutes

you will need for 4 servings:

1 cauliflower	½ pint basic white
2 eggs, hard-	sauce (see page 82)
boiled	chopped parsley

1 Break the cauliflower up into flowerets and cook in boiling salted water until just tender.
2 Drain well, and put into a hot dish with the sliced hard-boiled egg, saving a little egg yolk for garnish – keep hot.
3 Make the sauce, season carefully and pour over the cauliflower and egg.
4 Decorate with the sieved hard-boiled egg yolk and chopped parsley.

Celery and tomato sauce

cooking time: about 20 minutes

you will need for 4 servings:

1–2 heads celery,	1 teaspoon lemon
according to size	juice
½ pint cheese sauce	3–4 tomatoes, peeled
(see page 83)	and sliced
3 oz. grated cheese	chopped parsley
1 oz. butter	

1 Prepare the celery, cut into about 2-in. lengths and cook in boiling salted water.
2 Make the cheese sauce, using some of the water in which the celery was cooked, if liked.

3 Add butter, most of the cheese, lemon juice and drained celery. Correct the seasoning.
4 Put into a greased fireproof dish. Sprinkle the rest of the cheese on top and arrange slices of tomato round the edge.
5 Brown under a hot grill or in the oven.
6 Sprinkle parsley on top.

Cauliflower with quick curry sauce

cooking time: 20–25 minutes

you will need for 4 servings:

1 cauliflower	1 oz. flour
chicken stock or	1 level tablespoon
water	curry powder
1 oz. butter	2 oz. sultanas
1 small onion, peeled	1 hard-boiled egg
and chopped	

1 Prepare the cauliflower, divide into flowerets and cook in chicken stock or salted water. Drain and retain the liquid.
2 Meanwhile, melt the butter, add the onion and sauté until soft but not coloured.
3 Add the flour and the curry powder, mix well and stir over a gentle heat for 5 minutes.
4 Remove from the heat, add ½ pint of the liquid and stir until smooth.
5 Return to the heat and boil for 3 minutes stirring all the time.
6 Add the sultanas and chopped hard-boiled egg. Correct the seasoning and pour over the cauliflower.

Cabbage and potato pie

cooking time: about 30 minutes

you will need for 4 servings:

1 lb. cooked cold	1 lb. cooked, well-
potatoes	drained cabbage
4–6 oz. rashers	little milk
streaky bacon	1 oz. butter

1 Slice the potatoes and put a layer into the bottom of a well greased fireproof dish.
2 Add some of the rashers, cut into pieces.
3 Cover with a layer of chopped cabbage.
4 Repeat the layers until all the ingredients are used up, finishing up with potato.
5 Pour over enough milk to moisten.
6 Dot with butter and bake about 30 minutes in a moderate oven (350°F – Gas Mark 4).

Poached eggs on cabbage

cooking time: 15–20 minutes

you will need for 4 servings:

1 medium-sized firm-hearted cabbage	salt and pepper
¼ pint basic white sauce (see page 82)	1–2 tablespoons tomato purée
	4 eggs, poached

1 Remove the outer leaves of the cabbage, cut into quarters and remove the hard stalk. Wash well, then shred finely.
2 Cook in boiling salted water until tender, then drain thoroughly.
3 Make the white sauce, add seasoning and tomato purée.
4 Reheat the cabbage in the sauce. Put into a shallow serving dish and arrange the poached eggs on top.

Broad beans with bacon

cooking time: about 20 minutes

you will need for 4 servings:

8–10 spring onions	2 lb. broad beans
4 oz. lean bacon	½ pint white stock
1 oz. butter	salt and pepper
2 level teaspoons flour	chopped parsley

1 Cut the onions into two or three pieces, cut the bacon into strips.
2 Fry lightly in the butter until the onion is soft, but not coloured.
3 Add the flour and mix in well.
4 Add the beans and stock, stir until boiling, then cook slowly until the beans are tender.
5 Correct the seasoning and turn into a serving dish. Sprinkle the top with parsley.

Celery tart

cooking time: 15–20 minutes

you will need for 4 servings:

1 can celery hearts	1 tablespoon white wine
¼ pint cheese sauce (see page 83)	pepper
1 oz. butter	1 8-in. baked pastry case (see page 87)
1 tablespoon thin cream or top of milk	2 tablespoons grated cheese

1 Drain the celery and chop finely.
2 Add to the cheese sauce with the butter, cream, wine and pepper to taste. Beat all well together.
3 Pour into the pastry case, sprinkle with cheese

and bake about 15 minutes in a very moderate oven (335°F – Gas Mark 3).

Stuffed vegetable marrow

cooking time: 25–30 minutes

you will need for 4 servings:

1 medium-sized marrow	1 teaspoon chopped parsley
3 tablespoons chopped cooked meat	little grated lemon rind
	1 egg
3 tablespoons breadcrumbs	salt and pepper

1 Wash and peel the marrow, cut through lengthways and remove the seeds.
2 Mix the meat, breadcrumbs, parsley and lemon rind together.
3 Bind with the egg and season carefully.
4 Put the filling on half the marrow and cover with the other half.
5 Put into a greased fireproof dish, cover and bake in a moderately hot oven (375°F – Gas Mark 5).

Marrow savoury

cooking time: 25 minutes

you will need for 4 servings:

equal quantities of cooked marrow, cooked rice and cooked potato, about 1 cup of each	4 oz. grated cheese
	salt and pepper
	2 oz. butter

1 Mixed the diced marrow, rice and diced potato together with about 1 oz. cheese. Season carefully.
2 Put a layer into a greased fireproof dish, sprinkle with some of the remaining cheese and a few flakes of butter.
3 Add another layer of vegetables, sprinkle with cheese and continue until the ingredients are used up, finishing with grated cheese and flakes of butter.
4 Bake for about 20 minutes in a moderate oven (350°F – Gas Mark 4).

Savoury marrow rings

cooking time: 20–25 minutes

you will need for 4 servings:

1 medium-sized marrow	2 hard-boiled eggs
3 tablespoons breadcrumbs	1 oz. walnuts
	salt and pepper
1 tablespoon milk	nutmeg
3 oz. grated cheese	1 egg

1 Peel the marrow and cut into rings about 1–1½ inches thick removing the seeds. Arrange in a greased fireproof dish.

2 Put the breadcrumbs into a basin with the milk. Leave for a few minutes to soak.

3 Add the cheese, reserving a little, chopped hard-boiled eggs and chopped nuts.

4 Add salt and pepper and a good pinch of nutmeg. Bind with beaten egg.

5 Put this mixture into the centre of each ring of marrow. Sprinkle with remaining cheese and bake for about 20 minutes in a moderately hot oven (375°F – Gas Mark 5).

Celery and apple flan

cooking time: 20–25 minutes

you will need for 4 servings:

1 can celery hearts	2–3 rashers bacon
salt and pepper	1 teaspoon cornflour
1 large cooking apple	2 eggs
1 7-in. baked flan case (see page 87)	1 tablespoon grated cheese

1 Drain the celery well. Chop and put into the baked flan case. Add a little salt and pepper.

2 Peel, core and chop the apple and sprinkle on top of the celery.

3 Cut the bacon into strips and put into the flan case.

4 Mix the cornflour smoothly with the beaten eggs, season and pour on top.

5 Sprinkle with the cheese and bake about 20 minutes in a moderately hot oven (375°F – Gas Mark 5).

Mushroom and cheese flan

cooking time: about 20 minutes

you will need for 4 servings:

1 small onion, peeled and chopped	3 oz. grated cheese
4 oz. mushrooms, sliced	1 tablespoon chopped parsley
2 oz. butter	1 8-in. baked pastry case (see page 87)
½ pint basic white sauce (see page 82)	2–3 tomatoes, peeled and sliced

1 Fry the onion and mushrooms in the butter.

2 Make the sauce, add the cheese, parsley and onion and mushroom mixture. Correct the seasoning.

3 Pour into the pastry case.

4 Arrange slices of tomato round edge, bake in a moderate oven (350°F – Gas Mark 4).

Leeks au gratin

cooking time: 20–25 minutes

you will need for 4 servings:

7–8 leeks	½ level teaspoon made mustard
2 oz. butter	
2 oz. cornflour	lemon juice
½ pint milk	2 tablespoons breadcrumbs
4 oz. grated cheese, Gruyère or Cheddar	little butter
salt and black pepper	

1 Prepare and wash the leeks thoroughly then cook in boiling salted water until just tender. Drain and put into a greased fireproof dish.

2 Melt the butter, add the cornflour and mix well. Cook for a few minutes, then remove from the heat.

3 Add the milk gradually, return to the heat, stir until boiling and boil for 1 minute.

4 Add cheese and continue cooking until it has melted, then season carefully with salt, pepper, mustard and a squeeze of lemon juice.

5 Pour the sauce over the leeks, sprinkle with the breadcrumbs and dot with butter.

6 Bake in a moderate oven (350°F – Gas Mark 4) until the top is golden brown.

Cheese and vegetable pie

cooking time: about 30 minutes

you will need for 4 servings:

1 lb. parboiled potatoes	salt and pepper
2 medium-sized onions	4 tablespoons thin cream or milk
8 oz. Cheddar cheese	butter

1 Slice the potatoes and put a layer into a well greased casserole.

2 Cover with half the onion, finely chopped, and then add a layer of cheese, sliced as thinly as possible.

3 Repeat the layers, seasoning each one.

4 Moisten with the cream or milk and cover with the last layer of potatoes.

5 Dot with butter, cover and bake for about 20 minutes in a moderate oven (350°F – Gas Mark 4).

6 Remove the lid and continue cooking until the potatoes are brown.

Mixed vegetable pie

cooking time: 20–25 minutes

you will need for 4 servings:

1 lb. mixed cooked vegetables (carrots, peas, beans, etc., as available)	½ pint cheese sauce (see page 83)
1–2 tomatoes, peeled and sliced	1 lb. cooked mashed potato, well seasoned
1 hard-boiled egg, sliced	1 tablespoon grated cheese
	½ oz. butter

1 Mix the vegetables, tomatoes, and egg together with the sauce.
2 Put into a fireproof dish and cover with the potato.
3 Sprinkle with grated cheese and dot with butter.
4 Bake for about 20 minutes in a moderately hot oven (375°F – Gas Mark 5).

Tomato surprise

cooking time: 10–15 minutes

you will need for 4 servings:

4 large, firm tomatoes	1 dessertspoon breadcrumbs
2 large mushrooms	salt and pepper
1 oz. butter	4 eggs

1 Cut a slice from the stalk of each tomato and carefully scoop out the pulp. Remove the seeds and chop the pulp.
2 Chop the mushrooms and fry in the butter.
3 Add the tomato pulp, breadcrumbs and salt and pepper and mix all well.
4 Put a little of this mixture into each tomato case.
5 Break the eggs carefully and drop one into each tomato case.
6 Add a little salt and pepper and bake in a moderate oven (350°F – Gas Mark 4) until the egg is lightly set.

Stuffed tomatoes

cooking time: 15–20 minutes

you will need for 4 servings:

4 large firm tomatoes	1 tablespoon chopped cooked ham
2 tablespoons breadcrumbs	salt and pepper
2 tablespoons grated cheese	½ oz. butter
little chopped parsley	4 rounds of buttered toast

1 Cut a slice from the stalk end of each tomato and remove the pulp.
2 To the pulp, add the breadcrumbs, cheese, ham and parsley and season carefully.
3 Re-fill the tomato cases, sprinkle a few breadcrumbs on top and add a small knob of butter.
4 Bake about 15 minutes in a moderate oven 350°F – Gas Mark 4).
5 Serve on the rounds of buttered toast.

Tomato and spaghetti bake

cooking time: 25–30 minutes

you will need:

8 oz. tomatoes, peeled and sliced	3 oz. grated cheese
salt and pepper	½ pint white sauce (see page 82)
pinch tarragon	1 egg
4 oz. cooked spaghetti	

1 Put half the tomatoes into a greased fireproof dish. Add salt and pepper, a pinch of sugar and a pinch of chopped tarragon if available.
2 Cover with half the spaghetti and half the cheese.
3 Repeat the layers finishing with cheese, reserving a little to sprinkle over the dish before baking.
4 Make up the white sauce, allow to cool a little then add the beaten egg.
5 Pour the sauce over the top and sprinkle with the remaining cheese.
6 Bake for about 25 minutes in a very moderate oven (335°F – Gas Mark 3).

Scalloped tomatoes

cooking time: 20–25 minutes

you will need for 4 servings:

4 oz. breadcrumbs	1 lb. tomatoes, peeled and sliced
2 medium-sized onions, peeled and chopped	pinch sugar
2 oz. butter	1 tablespoon grated cheese
salt and pepper	

1 Grease a pie dish and sprinkle a layer of breadcrumbs in the bottom.
2 Cook the onion in a little of the butter until soft and lightly browned.
3 Put half the tomatoes into the dish, sprinkle with salt and pepper and a pinch of sugar.
4 Add half the onion.

5 Repeat the layers, reserving 1 tablespoon breadcrumbs.
6 Mix the remaining breadcrumbs with the cheese and sprinkle on top.
7 Dot with the remaining butter and bake for 20–25 minutes in a moderate oven (350°F – Gas Mark 4).

Tomato and cheese flan

cooking time: 25–30 minutes

you will need for 4 servings:

4–5 tomatoes, peeled and sliced	1 small onion, peeled and chopped
1 8-in. baked pastry case (see page 87)	2 eggs
1 oz. butter	¾ pint milk
	salt and pepper
	4 oz. grated cheese

1 Put the tomatoes into the pastry case.
2 Fry the onion in the butter and sprinkle over the tomatoes.
3 Beat the eggs, add the milk, seasoning and most of the cheese.
4 Pour into the pastry case and sprinkle with the remaining cheese.
5 Bake in a moderate oven (350°F – Gas Mark 4) until firm and lightly browned.

Savoury patties

cooking time: about 25 minutes

you will need for 4 servings:

6 oz. rough puff or flaky pastry (see page 86)	1 tablespoon breadcrumbs
2 tomatoes, peeled and chopped	2 oz. grated cheese
1 small onion, peeled and chopped	salt and pepper
	1 egg

1 Roll the pastry thinly and divide into 6 portions.
2 Mix the tomatoes, onion, breadcrumbs and cheese together, season and bind with the beaten egg.
3 Divide this mixture equally between the 6 pieces of pastry. Damp the edges and fold over, pressing the edges well together. Decorate the edge as liked.
4 Make an incision in the top of the pastry to allow the steam to escape and bake for 10 minutes in a hot oven (425°F – Gas Mark 7), then reduce the heat to 350°F – Gas Mark 4 for a further 15 minutes.

Tomato and cheese savoury

cooking time: about 30 minutes

you will need for 4 servings:

1 oz. butter	cayenne pepper
¾ oz. flour	½ level teaspoon sugar
¼ pint canned tomato juice	2 eggs
salt and pepper	2 tablespoons grated cheese

1 Melt the butter, add the flour and mix well. Add tomato juice, stir until boiling and cook for 3 minutes stirring all the time.
2 Add seasonings and sugar.
3 Add egg yolks and cheese.
4 Beat the egg whites until stiff and fold into the mixture.
5 Pour into a greased fireproof dish and bake in a moderate oven (350°F – Gas Mark 4) for about 30 minutes.

Sweet corn soufflé

cooking time: about 20 minutes

you will need for 4 servings:

2 oz. butter	1 teaspoon sugar
½ green pepper, finely chopped	salt and pepper
1 small onion, peeled and chopped	¼ pint milk
	4 tablespoons water
1 can creamed sweet corn	2 whole eggs
	1 egg white

1 Melt the butter in a pan, add the pepper and onion and cook until soft but not brown.
2 Add the corn, sugar and seasoning and mix well.
3 Add the milk and water, stir until boiling and cook for a few minutes.
4 Remove from the heat, beat in the egg yolks, then fold in the 3 stiffly beaten whites.
5 Put into a deep greased baking dish and bake in a hot oven (425°F – Gas Mark 7).

Spinach and mushroom savoury

cooking time: about 15 minutes

you will need for 4 servings:

2 lb. spinach	4 oz. grated cheese
salt, pepper, nutmeg	1 tablespoon breadcrumbs
8 oz. mushrooms	½ oz. butter
½ pint basic white sauce (see page 82)	

1 Cook the spinach, drain thoroughly and then chop finely. *continued*

2 Add salt, pepper and nutmeg to the spinach and put it into a fireproof dish.
3 Slice the mushrooms thinly and place on top.
4 Make up the white sauce, add 3 oz. of the cheese and correct the seasoning.
5 Pour over the mushrooms, mix the remaining cheese and breadcrumbs together and sprinkle on top.
6 Dot with butter and put into a moderate oven (350°F – Gas Mark 4) for about 15 minutes.

Spinach soufflé

cooking time: 30 minutes

you will need for 4 servings:

½ pint cooked spinach	salt and pepper
2 oz. butter	nutmeg
2 oz. flour	3 eggs
½ pint milk	

1 The spinach must be well drained and very finely chopped or sieved.
2 Melt the butter, add the flour and cook for a few minutes.
3 Remove from the heat and stir in the milk.
4 Return to the heat, stir until boiling and boil for 3 minutes stirring all the time.
5 Add the spinach and season very well with salt, pepper and a pinch of nutmeg.
6 Stir in the egg yolks and fold in the stiffly beaten egg whites.
7 Put into a soufflé dish or deep baking dish and bake in a moderately hot oven (375°F – Gas Mark 5).

Spinach Louise

cooking time: 15–20 minutes

you will need for 4 servings:

1 lb. cooked mashed potato	2 tablespoons thin cream or top of the milk
little milk or egg	
2 lb. spinach	4 oz. cooked ham, diced
salt and pepper	
nutmeg	3 hard-boiled eggs, sliced

1 Arrange the potato round the edge of a shallow fireproof dish, brush with milk or egg and put into a moderately hot oven (375°F – Gas Mark 5) to brown, while the rest of the dish is prepared.
2 Prepare and cook spinach for about 7–10 minutes.

3 Drain well and chop it roughly, season with salt, freshly ground pepper and a pinch of nutmeg.
4 Add the cream and carefully stir in the ham and eggs.
5 Put into the potato-lined dish and serve hot sprinkled with parsley.

Spinach with eggs and noodles

cooking time: about 25 minutes

you will need for 4 servings:

8 oz. noodles	4 eggs
½ oz. butter	¼ pint cheese sauce (see page 83)
8 oz. cooked spinach or use 1 carton frozen spinach	1 tablespoon grated cheese

1 Cook the noodles in boiling salted water for 10 minutes. Drain and add the butter, then put into a shallow fireproof dish.
2 Spread the cooked spinach on top.
3 Make four nests in the spinach and break one egg in each. Season with salt and pepper.
4 Pour the sauce over the eggs, sprinkle with cheese and bake about 25 minutes in a moderate oven (350°F – Gas Mark 4).

Risotto

cooking time: 25–30 minutes

you will need for 4 servings:

1 medium-sized onion, peeled and chopped	1 oz. cooked mushrooms, sliced
2 oz. butter	2 oz. cooked ham, chopped
6 oz. Patna rice	½ small red pepper, blanched and chopped
1 pint chicken stock	
2 tablespoons cooked green peas	seasoning

1 Fry the onion in the butter until lightly browned.
2 Add the rice and mix well.
3 Add the stock, bring to boiling point, cover and cook until the rice is tender and most of the stock is absorbed.
4 Add all the other ingredients and continue cooking for about 5 minutes.

Hungarian hot pot

cooking time: 25–30 minutes

you will need for 4 servings:

1 lb. cooked potatoes	3 hard-boiled eggs,
4 oz. rashers streaky	sliced
bacon	1 tablespoon
¼ pint yoghourt	breadcrumbs
or sour milk	½ oz. butter

1 Slice the potatoes and put half of them into a greased fireproof dish.
2 Cover with half the bacon rashers and then pour on half the yoghourt and cover with half the eggs.
3 Continue in layers finishing with potatoes.
4 Sprinkle with crumbs and dot with butter.
5 Put into a moderate oven (350°F – Gas Mark 4) to brown.

Potato croquettes

cooking time: 5–7 minutes to fry

you will need for 4 servings:

1 lb. cooked	2 oz. minced cooked
potatoes	meat
1 oz. butter	salt and pepper
2 oz. grated cheese	1 egg
pinch mixed herbs	egg and breadcrumbs

1 Warm the potatoes in a pan with the butter and beat until creamy.
2 Add cheese, meat, herbs and seasonings and bind with beaten egg.
3 Turn on to a floured board and using floured hands, shape into croquettes.
4 Coat with egg and breadcrumbs and fry in hot fat until crisp and golden.

Potato bake

cooking time: 25 minutes

you will need for 4 servings:

1 packet mushroom	1 oz. breadcrumbs
soup	3 oz. grated Cheddar
3–4 oz. streaky bacon	cheese
1 lb. boiled potatoes	

1 Make up mushroom soup.
2 Chop bacon roughly and fry for 5 minutes.
3 Slice potatoes and place half in a greased baking dish. Sprinkle bacon over potatoes. Add remaining potatoes.
4 Pour in soup – about 1 pint will be required.
5 Mix breadcrumbs and cheese. Sprinkle over the top layer of potatoes.
6 Bake in a hot oven (400°F – Gas Mark 6) for 15–20 minutes until heated through.

Parsnip and potato cakes

cooking time: 5–7 minutes

you will need for 4 servings:

8 oz. cooked parsnips	1 egg yolk
8 oz. boiled potatoes	1 tablespoon thin
salt and pepper	cream or top of milk
pinch brown sugar	egg and breadcrumbs
1 tablespoon chopped	for coating
parsley	

1 Rub the parsnips and potatoes through a sieve.
2 Add seasoning, sugar and parsley, and bind with egg yolk and cream.
3 Shape into rissoles, coat with egg and breadcrumbs and fry in hot fat until crisp and golden.
4 These are very good served with grilled rashers of bacon.

Stuffed peppers

cooking time: 20 minutes

you will need for 4 servings:

4 good-sized peppers	1 4-oz. can shrimps
– red or green	salt and pepper
1 small onion	lemon juice
1 oz. butter	½ pint stock
4 oz. cooked rice	

1 Wash the peppers, cut off the tops and remove the seeds and pith.
2 Peel and chop the onion finely.
3 Fry in the butter until soft.
4 Add rice and shrimps and season carefully adding lemon juice to taste.
5 Pile into the peppers and put into a greased fireproof dish.
6 Pour the stock over and bake about 20 minutes in a moderate oven (350°F – Gas Mark 4).

Onion pasty

cooking time: 25–30 minutes

you will need for 4 servings:

12 oz. onions	2 tablespoons stock
3 oz. grated cheese	or gravy
3–4 tomatoes	8 oz. short crust
salt and pepper	pastry (see page 86)

1 Mince or chop the onion very finely.
2 Add grated cheese and tomatoes peeled and chopped. *continued*

3 Season carefully and add the stock.
4 Roll the pastry into an oblong shape. Put the filling on half, moisten the edges and fold over.
5 Press the edges well together and decorate as liked.
6 Put on to a baking tray, brush with egg or milk and bake in a moderately hot oven (375°F – Gas Mark 5).

Cheese and onion tart

cooking time: 25–30 minutes

you will need for 4 servings:

2 oz. butter	2 eggs
4 oz. onions, peeled and thinly sliced	6 oz. grated cheese
1 oz. flour	1 8-in. baked pastry case
½ pint milk	(see page 87)
salt and pepper	

1 Melt the butter and fry the onion until soft but not coloured.
2 Stir in the flour and mix well.
3 Add the milk, stir until boiling and boil for 3 minutes. Add seasoning.
4 Cool a little, then stir in the egg yolks and most of the cheese, reheat without boiling.
5 Beat the egg whites until stiff and fold into the sauce mixture.
6 Pour into the pastry case, sprinkle with the remaining cheese and bake for about 25 minutes in a moderate oven (350°F – Gas Mark 4).

Salads

The recipes in the following chapter will, I think, help to put to shame those pieces of tired lettuce and tomato which too often masquerade under the name of 'salad'. And even if some of the ingredients and combinations do seem a bit unusual, I hope you will still be willing to try them. I feel sure you will find it well worth the effort.

Russian salad

you will need for 4 servings:

1–2 cooked carrots, diced	2 tablespoons cooked French beans, cut into pieces
1–2 cooked potatoes, diced	½ small cooked beetroot, diced
2 tablespoons cooked green peas	mayonnaise (see page 82)
	1 gherkin, chopped
	3–4 anchovy fillets

1 Put all the vegetables together in a bowl.
2 Add enough mayonnaise to moisten well.
3 Put into a salad bowl and garnish with the gherkin and anchovy fillets.

California coleslaw

you will need:

½ packet white onion soup mix	2 oz. carrot, grated
2 cartons sour cream	½ green pepper, chopped
¼ white cabbage, shredded	1 tablespoon cider vinegar

To garnish:
½ green pepper, in strips

1 Mix the contents of the packet of onion soup with the soured cream. Stir in the other ingredients.
2 Chill overnight.
3 Serve garnished with thin strips of green pepper.

Salad Niçoise

you will need for 4 servings:

½ small clove garlic	2 hard-boiled eggs, sliced
½ lettuce	1 7-oz. can tuna fish
1 head chicory	French dressing (see page 82)
2 tomatoes, peeled and quartered	1 small can anchovy fillets
small pieces cucumber, sliced	few black olives, optional

1 Rub round the salad bowl with the cut clove of garlic.
2 Shred the lettuce, divide the spears of chicory and put into the salad bowl with the tomatoes, cucumber and eggs.
3 Drain excess oil from the fish, divide into 4 portions and put on top of the salad.
4 Pour over the dressing and garnish with anchovy fillets and olives.

Portuguese salad

you will need for 4 servings:

1 can tuna fish	8 oz. cooked French
3–4 olives	beans
pepper	3–4 tomatoes, peeled
lemon juice	and sliced
8 oz. cooked new	1 head chicory
potatoes, sliced	

For the dressing:

1 level teaspoon dry	2 tablespoons oil
mustard	salt and pepper
1 tablespoon white	
vinegar	

1 Drain excess oil from fish, flake finely and mix with the chopped olives. Add lemon juice and pepper to taste.
2 Arrange the potatoes, beans and tomatoes in layers on a serving dish.
3 Pile the fish on top.
4 Mix the mustard smoothly with the vinegar, add the oil and seasoning and pour this dressing over the fish.
5 Divide the chicory into spears and use to garnish the salad.

Palermo salad

you will need for 4 servings:

1 small lettuce	1 good tablespoon
2 tablespoons diced,	mayonnaise (see
cooked carrots	page 82)
2 tablespoons cooked	lemon juice
green peas	little made mustard
2 tablespoons cooked	4–6 slices cooked ham
rice	

1 Line a shallow serving dish with the lettuce.
2 Mix the carrots, peas and rice together, and season as required.
3 Mix the mayonnaise with a squeeze of lemon juice and a little mustard.
4 Add the vegetables to the mayonnaise and mix well.
5 Put a good spoonful of the mixture on each slice of ham and roll up or just fold in half.
6 Arrange on the lettuce and garnish as liked with olives or tomato wedges.

Danish salad

you will need for 4 servings:

1 lettuce	2 small apples, peeled,
4 cooked herrings,	cored and diced
preferably soused	3–4 cooked potatoes,
1 cooked beetroot,	diced
peeled and diced	French dressing (see
	page 82)

For garnish:

1 small apple	chopped parsley
little lemon juice	

1 Arrange the lettuce on a shallow serving dish.
2 Remove skin and bones from the fish and flake finely.
3 Mix with the beetroot, diced apples and potatoes.
4 Toss lightly in the dressing and pile on top of the lettuce.
5 Core but do not peel the apple, cut into slices, dip in lemon juice and place round the fish mixture.
6 Sprinkle with parsley before serving.

Cabbage salad

you will need for 4 servings:

½ small firm cabbage	½ small onion
1 head celery	salad cream (see page
1 apple	82)
2 oz. walnuts	2 tomatoes

1 Prepare the cabbage and shred finely.
2 Wash and remove outer leaves of celery, chop the heart.
3 Chop the apple, nuts and onion.
4 Mix all ingredients together and bind with a little salad cream.
5 Put into a bowl and garnish with wedges of tomato.

Pineapple and lettuce salad

you will need for 4 servings:

1 lettuce	salt and pepper
3 tablespoons oil	pinch of sugar
1 tablespoon vinegar	2 teaspoons finely
1 tablespoon	chopped parsley
pineapple juice	½ small can pineapple

1 Prepare the lettuce and shred it.
2 Mix the oil, vinegar, pineapple juice, seasoning and sugar together, toss the lettuce in it, then remove and arrange round the edge of a salad bowl.
3 Dice the pineapple and put into the centre of the bowl.
4 Add the parsley to the remaining dressing and pour over the pineapple.

Moulded grapefruit salad

you will need for 4 servings:

1 16-oz. can	1 dessert apple,
grapefruit	peeled and chopped
½ oz. gelatine	2–3 sticks celery,
2 tablespoons lemon	chopped
juice	

1 Drain the syrup from the grapefruit and make the quantity up to $\frac{1}{2}$ pint with water.
2 Dissolve the gelatine in a little of the syrup over hot water, then add to the rest of the syrup. Add lemon juice and leave until it just begins to get syrupy.
3 Fold in the grapefruit segments, apple and celery.
4 Pour into a mould and turn out when set.

Honeyed salad

you will need for 4 servings:

For dressing:

1 tablespoon thin honey	3 tablespoons lemon juice

For salad:

8 oz. dessert apples	8 oz. cooked carrots
2 oz. seedless raisins	2 oz. mixed nuts

1 Mix the honey and lemon juice together.
2 Peel and core the apples and cut into dice.
3 Add the raisins, chopped nuts and sliced carrots.
4 Mix with the dressing and leave in a cool place for an hour before using.

Note

Serve this salad with galantines or with cold turkey.

Cucumber salad

you will need for 4 servings:

$\frac{1}{4}$ large or 1 small cucumber	2 tablespoons French dressing (see page 82)
salt	
1 teaspoon finely chopped parsley	

1 The cucumber can be peeled or not as preferred. Cut into thin slices, put on to a dish and sprinkle with salt. Leave to stand for an hour if possible, then drain off surplus water.
2 Arrange the cucumber in the serving dish, pour the dressing over and sprinkle parsley.

Bean and apple salad

you will need for 4 servings:

4 oz. cooked broad beans	salt
1 small dessert apple, sliced finely	4 tablespoons mayonnaise or salad cream (see page 82)
2–3 tablespoons raw white cabbage, shredded	1 hard-boiled egg
	1–2 pickled walnuts

1 Mix the beans with the apple and cabbage and season with a little salt.
2 Put into a serving dish and coat with the mayonnaise.
3 Garnish with slices of hard-boiled egg and walnuts.

Beetroot baskets

you will need for 4 servings:

4 medium-sized beetroots (cooked and left whole)	1 tablespoon finely diced cooked potatoes
1 teaspoon chopped chives	1 tablespoon chopped pickled walnuts
1 level teaspoon chopped mint	mayonnaise or salad cream (see page 82)

1 Cut a piece off the top of each beetroot, and using a small teaspoon scoop out the centre.
2 Chop the scooped out beetroot and mix with the other ingredients.
3 Bind with a little mayonnaise and then pile up well in the beetroot cases.

Cheese and pineapple salad

you will need for 4 servings:

1 tablespoon thick cream	lettuce
1 teaspoon lemon juice	1 small can pineapple rings
salt and cayenne pepper	1 tablespoon chopped walnuts
4 oz. cream or cottage cheese	red pepper

1 Partly whip the cream, add lemon juice and seasoning.
2 Add the cheese and mash up with the dressing.
3 Arrange the lettuce on a serving dish, cut up the pineapple and put on top.
4 Pile the cheese on top of the pineapple and sprinkle with the nuts and a little red pepper.

Apple and carrot salad

you will need for 4 servings:

lettuce	2 tablespoons thick cream
2 dessert apples	2 teaspoons lemon juice
2–3 raw carrots	salt and pepper
1 tablespoon seedless raisins	

1 Prepare some lettuce and line a small shallow salad bowl.
2 Chop the apple, grate the carrot and add the raisins.

3 Half whip the cream, add lemon juice and seasoning.

4 Add the apple mixture, blend lightly together and serve on the bed of lettuce.

Celery and beetroot salad

you will need for 4 servings:

small clove garlic	3 tablespoons diced
1 dessertspoon oil	cooked beetroot
2 teaspoons lemon	1 tablespoon chopped
juice	walnuts
salt and pepper	chopped parsley,
pinch of sugar	chervil or chives
3 tablespoons	
chopped celery	

1 Crush the garlic and rub it round a mixing bowl.

2 Put the oil and lemon juice into the bowl, add seasoning and sugar and blend well together.

3 Add the celery, beetroot and nuts and toss all together.

4 Put into a serving dish and sprinkle with parsley or other herbs.

Tomato salad

you will need for 4 servings:

1 lb. firm tomatoes	French dressing (see
pinch sugar	page 82)
2 spring onions or a	chopped parsley
little chopped raw	
onion	

1 Peel and slice the tomatoes and arrange on a flat serving dish. Add a pinch of sugar.

2 Sprinkle with the onion and pour on dressing.

3 Sprinkle with parsley before serving.

Cauliflower and bean salad

you will need for 4 servings:

1 small or ½	3–4 tablespoons
cauliflower	mayonnaise (see
8 oz. cooked broad	page 82)
beans	1 teaspoon finely
2 teaspoons minced	grated horseradish
or finely chopped	*or*
onion	2 teaspoons prepared
	horseradish cream
	cress

1 Prepare the cauliflower and divide into small flowerets.

2 Mix with the beans and onion.

3 Put the mayonnaise into a bowl and add the horseradish. Add the vegetables and toss all lightly together.

4 Put into a serving dish and garnish with the cress.

Tasmanian salad

you will need for 4 servings:

small piece of	4 tomatoes
cucumber	salt and pepper
2–3 celery sticks	French dressing (see
2 dessert apples	page 82)
2 bananas	lettuce
lemon juice	

1 Dice the cucumber and celery.

2 Peel and slice the apples and bananas and sprinkle with lemon juice.

3 Slice the tomatoes and sprinkle with salt and pepper.

4 Mix all the ingredients together and pour a little salad dressing over.

5 Arrange the lettuce in a bowl and pile the rest of the mixture on top.

Cream cheese and orange salad

you will need for 4 servings:

lettuce	1 carton cottage
watercress	cheese
small piece cucumber	2 oz. chopped nuts
2–3 oranges	French dressing (see
few grapes	page 82)

1 Arrange the lettuce, watercress and sliced cucumber in a salad bowl.

2 Peel the oranges, divide into segments and put in a circle with the grapes.

3 Mix the cheese with the nuts, roll into balls and arrange with the other ingredients.

4 Add the dressing just before serving.

Fruit and cheese salad

you will need for 4 servings:

1 carton cottage	1 lettuce
cheese	1 grapefruit
2 oz. walnuts,	2 bananas
chopped	French dressing (see
1–2 rings pineapple	page 82)

1 Mix the cheese with the nuts and pineapple.

2 Arrange the lettuce on a shallow dish reserving the heart for decorating. Pile the cheese in the centre.

3 Arrange the segments of grapefruit and slices of banana round the cheese, with pieces of the lettuce heart between.

4 Pour the dressing over the top.

Celery and cream cheese salad

you will need for 4 servings:

lettuce	1 tablespoon lemon
1–2 heads celery	juice
4 oz. cream cheese	salt and pepper
2 tablespoons salad	1–2 gherkins
oil	

1 Arrange the lettuce in a salad bowl.
2 Cut the celery into strips and pile on top of the lettuce.
3 Mix the cream cheese with the oil and lemon juice. Add salt and pepper and the chopped gherkins.
4 Pour over the celery and decorate, if liked, with a few chopped nuts.

Cabbage and celery slaw

you will need for 4 servings:

4 oz. shredded raw	2 teaspoons minced
cabbage	onion
2 oz. shredded celery	mayonnaise (see page
2 oz. cooked potato	82)

1 Mix all the vegetables together and add enough mayonnaise to bind.
2 Toss lightly together and put into a serving bowl.

Crab salad

you will need for 4 servings:

lettuce	3–4 cooked new
watercress	potatoes, diced
3–4 firm tomatoes	mayonnaise (see page
1 small can crab or	82)
1 fresh crab	

1 Arrange the lettuce and watercress in a salad bowl and surround with thin wedges of tomato.
2 Mix the crab meat and potatoes together.
3 Add enough mayonnaise to moisten.
4 Pile on top of the lettuce.

Fish salad

you will need for 4 servings:

lettuce	$\frac{1}{4}$ pint mayonnaise
small piece of	(see page 82)
cucumber	1–2 gherkins, chopped
2 tomatoes	1 teaspoon capers,
watercress	chopped
12 oz. cold cooked	salt and pepper
fish	lemon juice

1 Prepare the salad plants.
2 Remove all skin and bone from the fish and flake finely. Bind with a little of the mayonnaise.
3 Add flavourings and seasonings.
4 Pile the fish in the centre of a serving dish, and coat with the remaining mayonnaise.
5 Put slices of cucumber round the edge, surround with lettuce and use the tomatoes and cress for garnish.

Grapefruit and shrimp salad

you will need for 4 servings:

lettuce	1 pint shrimps (fresh,
1 grapefruit	frozen or canned)
small piece of	French dressing
cucumber	(see page 82)

1 Arrange the lettuce in a shallow salad bowl.
2 Prepare the grapefruit and divide into sections.
3 Dice the cucumber and mix with the grapefruit.
4 Add the shrimps.
5 Add 2–3 tablespoons French dressing and toss all well together.
6 Pile on top of the lettuce and if fresh shrimps are used, garnish with one or two heads.

Salmon and shrimp mayonnaise

you will need for 4 servings:

1 small can salmon	2–3 tomatoes
1 4-oz. can shrimps	mayonnaise (see page
small piece of	82)
cucumber	lettuce

1 Flake the salmon and add the shrimps, reserving a few for garnish.
2 Slice the cucumber and tomatoes.
3 Mix some mayonnaise with the fish and put it into the centre of a serving dish lined with lettuce.
4 Arrange alternate slices of cucumber and tomato round the edge and use the remaining shrimps to garnish the fish.
5 Hand extra mayonnaise separately.

Prawn and egg salad

you will need for 4 servings:

endive or lettuce	few radishes
1 pint prawns (fresh,	capers
frozen or canned)	French dressing (see
3 hard-boiled eggs,	page 82)
sliced	

1 Arrange the endive or lettuce round a flat serving dish.
2 Arrange the prawns and slices of egg neatly in layers.
3 Garnish with radishes and capers and serve the dressing separately.

Apple and prawn salad

you will need for 4 servings:

lettuce
2 apples
2 hard-boiled eggs
few stuffed olives
few radishes
½ pint prawns (fresh, frozen or canned)
mayonnaise (see page 82)
lemon juice

1 Line a salad bowl with lettuce, reserving the heart for garnish.
2 Core but do not peel apples, cut into dice.
3 Slice the eggs, olives and some of the radishes but keep one or two for garnish.
4 Mix the prawns with the other ingredients and bind with mayonnaise.
5 Add a little lemon juice and seasoning, if required.
6 Pile on top of the lettuce and garnish with radishes and the lettuce heart.

Tuna and macaroni salad

you will need for 4 servings:

1 can tuna fish
8 oz. cooked macaroni
½ small cucumber, diced
1 tablespoon finely grated onion
1 tablespoon chopped parsley
mayonnaise (see page 82)
salt and pepper
lemon juice
lettuce
paprika and olives for garnish

1 Drain excess oil from the fish and break it up into flakes.
2 Mix with the macaroni, cucumber, onion and parsley.
3 Add enough mayonnaise to moisten, correct the seasoning and add the lemon juice to taste.
4 Arrange the lettuce in a dish, pile the fish mixture on top.
5 Garnish with paprika and olives.

Salmon cole slaw

you will need for 4 servings:

1 7½-oz. can salmon
½ small cucumber, peeled and diced
3 tablespoons salad cream (see page 82)
lemon juice
salt and pepper
1 small or ½ large Savoy cabbage
2 hard-boiled eggs
2 tomatoes

1 Flake the salmon, add cucumber and salad cream.
2 Season with lemon juice, pepper and salt as required.
3 Shred the cabbage and put into a serving dish.
4 Pile the fish on top and garnish with slices of hard-boiled egg and wedges of tomato.

Slimming salad

you will need for 4 servings:

1 lettuce
4–6 radishes
small piece cucumber
3–4 spring onions
1 small red or green pepper
2 oz. cream cheese
3–4 tablespoons yoghourt
black pepper
little onion juice

1 Prepare the lettuce and arrange in a salad bowl.
2 Slice the radishes, slice but do not peel cucumber.
3 Slice onions and cut pepper into thin shreds.
4 Mix radishes, cucumber, onions and pepper with the cream cheese.
5 Add the yoghourt to which a little freshly ground black pepper and onion juice has been added.
6 Pile on the top of the lettuce.

Slimming salad 2

you will need for 4 servings:

1 lettuce
2 tomatoes
3–4 uncooked mushrooms
2–3 chives or spring onions
3–4 radishes
3–4 oz. shrimps (fresh or 1 small can)
1 tablespoon chopped parsley

1 Line a shallow bowl with the lettuce.
2 Arrange the sliced tomatoes and mushrooms on top.
3 Sprinkle with chopped chives and add sliced radishes and shrimps.
4 Moisten with the following dressing and finally sprinkle with parsley.

Slimming salad dressing

you will need for 4 servings:

1 level teaspoon made
   mustard
black pepper
pinch cayenne pepper

pinch paprika pepper
juice 1 lemon
juice 1 orange
white wine vinegar

1 Mix the mustard, pepper, cayenne and paprika together.
2 Add the lemon and orange juice and vinegar to taste.

Slimming salad 3

you will need for 4 servings:

1 small head celery
2 hard-boiled eggs
1 carrot
3–4 radishes
small piece cucumber
1 level teaspoon
   paprika

2 teaspoons lemon
   juice
3 tablespoons
   yoghourt
black pepper
2 teaspoons finely
   chopped parsley

1 Shred the celery and put into a serving dish.
2 Slice the eggs and arrange on top.
3 Add the grated carrot and sliced radishes and unpeeled cucumber.
4 Mix the paprika smoothly with the lemon juice, add to the yoghourt with a little freshly ground black pepper and chopped parsley.
5 Pour over the salad.

Salad Americana

you will need for 4 servings:

1 lettuce
4 oz. cream cheese
1 oz. chopped walnuts
½ level teaspoon celery
   salt
1–2 sticks celery,
   chopped

2 tablespoons thin
   cream
1 dessertspoon lemon
   juice
1 orange

1 Arrange the lettuce in a fairly shallow bowl.
2 Mix together the cheese, walnuts, celery salt, celery, cream, lemon juice and pile in the centre of the lettuce.
3 Peel the orange, removing as much of the pith as possible.
4 Divide into segments and arrange round the salad.

Grapefruit and vegetable salad

you will need for 4 servings:

2 large grapefruit
2 tablespoons cooked
   green peas
2 tablespoons cooked,
   diced carrots
2 tablespoons cooked,
   diced French beans
1 teaspoon minced
   raw onion

1 tablespoon mashed,
   cooked potatoes
2 tablespoons
   mayonnaise
   (see page 82)
1 teaspoon tomato
   purée
watercress

1 Cut the grapefruit in halves, remove the pulp with a teaspoon, then remove as much of the pith as possible without breaking the skin.
2 Mix the grapefruit pulp with the peas, carrots, beans and onion.
3 Mix the potato, mayonnaise, tomato purée together and add to the vegetables.
4 Pile into the grapefruit cases and decorate with watercress.

With other vegetables: The vegetables for this salad can be varied according to which cooked vegetables are available.

Main meal salad

you will need for 4 servings:

1 head lettuce
2 hard-boiled eggs
4 tomatoes
4 oz. cooked ham
2 oz. tongue

2 oz. cooked chicken
4 oz. cheese
watercress
French dressing (see
   page 82)

1 Wash and dry the lettuce, and line the bottom of a fairly shallow salad bowl.
2 Cut the eggs into quarters and the tomatoes into wedges.
3 Cut the meat and cheese into strips.
4 Arrange the meat and cheese in little heaps on lettuce and eggs and tomatoes in between.
5 Put the watercress in the centre.
6 Serve with French dressing (see page 82).

Beef salad

you will need for 4 servings:

1 head lettuce
12 oz.–1 lb. cold
   cooked beef
2 apples
2 sticks celery
1–2 shallots, chopped
   finely

½ clove garlic,
   chopped finely
2 tablespoons parsley,
   chopped
3 tablespoons oil
1 tablespoon vinegar
salt, freshly ground
   black pepper

1 Prepare the lettuce and use to line a salad bowl.
2 In a large basin put the beef and cut into large dice, peeled, cored and diced apples, chopped celery, shallots, garlic and parsley.
3 Mix the oil, vinegar and seasoning together and pour over the contents of the basin.
4 Mix all well together and pile on top of the lettuce.

Cheese and ham salad

you will need for 4 servings:

1 head lettuce	1 tablespoon vinegar
8 oz. Gruyère cheese	salt, freshly ground
12 oz. ham	black pepper
3 tablespoons oil	chopped parsley

1 Prepare the lettuce.
2 Cut the cheese and ham into dice.
3 Make the dressing and pour over the cheese and ham. Leave to stand for an hour or so in the refrigerator if possible.
4 Pile on top of the lettuce and sprinkle with chopped parsley.

Spring salad

you will need for 4 servings:

4 oz. cooked cold meat	3–4 small cooked new potatoes
3–4 spring onions	mayonnaise (see page 82)
2 tablespoons cooked green peas	lettuce
2 cooked carrots	1 tomato

1 Cut the meat into small pieces and chop the onions.
2 Put into a basin with the peas and the other vegetables cut into dice.
3 Add sufficient mayonnaise to bind.
4 Put into a salad bowl, arrange leaves of lettuce round the edge.
5 Garnish with tomato.

Egg salad

you will need for 4 servings:

1 lettuce	5–6 sardines or anchovies
3 hard-boiled eggs	few radishes
5–6 tablespoons mayonnaise (see page 82)	watercress or mustard and cress

1 Prepare the lettuce and put into a fairly shallow salad bowl.

2 Cut the eggs in half lengthwise and arrange on the lettuce cut-side downwards.
3 Coat each with the mayonnaise.
4 Cut the anchovies or sardines into fillets and use with the radishes and cress as garnish.

Italian salad

you will need for 4 servings:

4 oz. cooked boiled rice	1 teaspoon finely chopped onion
1 tablespoon tomato purée	2–3 hard-boiled eggs
8 oz. cooked cold beef	1 tablespoon finely chopped parsley
salt and pepper	2–3 tablespoons French dressing
	little made mustard

1 Put the rice into a basin and mix with the tomato purée.
2 Add the beef, shredded, and the onion, and season with salt and pepper.
3 Arrange in a serving dish, put slices of hard-boiled egg round the side and sprinkle with parsley.
4 Just before serving pour over a little French dressing to which a small quantity of made mustard has been added.

Ravigote salad

you will need for 4 servings:

lettuce	3–4 tablespoons cooked green peas
3–4 tomatoes	French dressing (see page 82)
4 oz. ham	
4 oz. tongue	
3–4 sticks celery	

1 Prepare the lettuce, reserve the heart for garnishing and break up the rest into a salad bowl.
2 Peel and slice the tomatoes, cut the meat into strips and dice the celery.
3 Blend all the ingredients together with a little French dressing and put into the salad bowl.
4 Garnish with the heart of the lettuce.

Ham roll-ups

you will need for 4 servings:

1 endive or lettuce	1 small can crushed pineapple
6 oz. cream cheese	8 slices cooked ham
salt	French dressing (see page 82)
1 teaspoon lemon juice	
3–4 sticks celery, diced	

1 Arrange the endive on a large serving dish.
2 Mix the cream cheese with salt, lemon juice and celery.
3 Strain any excess juice from the pineapple, a little can be mixed with the cream cheese if liked but avoid making the mixture too soft.
4 Spread some of the cheese mixture on each slice of ham. Cover with a spoonful of pineapple and roll up. If necessary serve with a cocktail stick.
5 Toss the endive in a little dressing and arrange the rolls on top.

Chicken and ham salad

you will need for 4 servings:

6 oz. cooked diced chicken	salt and pepper
6 oz. cooked diced ham	2–4 tablespoons mayonnaise
6 oz. cooked rice	lettuce
2 dessert apples	2 tomatoes
2 oz. walnuts	small piece cucumber

1 Mix the chicken, ham and rice together.
2 Core the apples, but do not peel, slice thinly and put with the chicken.
3 Chop the walnuts and add to the other ingredients.
4 Season carefully then add the mayonnaise.
5 Pile on to a bed of lettuce and garnish with tomato and cucumber.

Luncheon salad 1

you will need for 4 servings:

1 lb. cooked potatoes	1 head lettuce
2–3 spring onions	4 cold cooked sausages
1 teaspoon chopped parsley	4 slices cooked ham
salad dressing (see page 82)	8 oz. tomatoes
	2 hard-boiled eggs

1 Dice the potatoes and mix with the chopped onion and parsley.
2 Add 1–2 tablespoons salad dressing, toss lightly and pile in the centre of a large flat dish.
3 Arrange lettuce round.
4 Put a sausage on to each slice of ham and roll up.
5 Arrange the ham rolls round the dish evenly.
6 Garnish with slices or wedges of tomato and egg.

Luncheon salad 2

you will need for 4 servings:

1 lettuce	2 tablespoons thin cream
3–4 dessert apples	12 oz. cooked ham or other cooked meat
lemon juice	
½ small green pepper	2 oz. Danish blue cheese
mayonnaise, about 4 tablespoons (see page 82)	

1 Line a salad bowl with the lettuce.
2 Reserve one apple for garnish, peel, core and slice the rest and sprinkle with lemon juice.
3 Cut the pepper into thin slices.
4 Mix the cream with the mayonnaise.
5 Mix the meat, cut into dice, apples and pepper and toss lightly in the mayonnaise.
6 Put into the salad bowl and crumble the cheese on top.
7 Garnish with slices of unpeeled apple.

Vegetarian salad 1

you will need for 4 servings:

1 lettuce	4 oz. cream cheese
2 large fresh pears or 1 small can	2 oz. chopped dates
	1 oz. chopped walnuts
lemon juice	seasoning

1 Prepare the lettuce, shred the outer leaves and keep the heart for garnish. Put the shredded lettuce on to a serving dish.
2 Peel and halve the pears, remove the core and a little of the flesh.
3 Sprinkle the pears with lemon juice.
4 Put the flesh cut from the pears into a bowl with the cheese, dates and nuts and mix well. Add seasoning as required.
5 Pile a little on each pear and roll the rest into small balls.
6 Arrange the pears and the balls on the lettuce and decorate with the heart of the lettuce.
7 Serve salad dressing separately.

Vegetarian salad 2

you will need for 4 servings:

1 lettuce	2 oz. seedless raisins
1 small head celery	1 oz. sultanas
2 apples	mayonnaise (see page 82)
2 oz. hazelnuts or walnuts	2 oz. grated cheese

1 Line a salad bowl with the lettuce.
2 Chop the celery, peel, core and chop the apples.

3 Mix the celery, apples, chopped nuts, raisins and sultanas together.
4 Add enough mayonnaise to moisten.

Puddings and Sweets

When you feel in the mood for providing a pudding or sweet with a main meal, there is no reason why you cannot do so, even if time is limited. You will find many imaginative ideas in the following chapter for delightful desserts which are both quick and easy to prepare.

Lemon raspberry sundae

cooking time: about 10 minutes

you will need for 4 servings:

1 oz. cornflour	3 tablespoons thin
5 oz. sugar	cream
2 eggs	fresh or frozen
½ pint milk	raspberries
2 lemons	

1 Mix the cornflour with 4 oz. sugar and blend to a thin cream with yolks and a little milk.
2 Heat the remaining milk with the thinly pared lemon rind.
3 Strain the milk on to the cornflour mixture, return to the heat, bring to the boil and allow to boil for 3 minutes, stirring.
4 Remove from heat, stir in lemon juice, then cream.
5 Beat egg whites until stiff, beat in remaining sugar.
6 Fold lightly into cooked mixture, chill well.
7 Arrange alternate layers of lemon mixture and raspberries in sundae glasses.
8 Serve with sponge or wafer biscuits, if liked.

Peach Melba sundae

no cooking

you will need for 4 servings:

1 large can peach slices	½ jar Melba sauce
2 × 5 oz. cartons natural yoghourt	4–5 digestive or macaroon biscuits

To decorate:
whipped cream

1 Drain the peaches and arrange in layers with the yoghourt, Melba sauce and crushed biscuits in tall sundae glasses.

5 Pile on top of the lettuce and sprinkle with grated cheese.

2 Finish with a layer of fruit and decorate with a rosette of whipped cream.
3 Chill before serving.

Strawberry cream flan

no cooking

you will need for 4 servings:

1 10-oz. block ice cream	1 sponge flan case fresh strawberries
1 strawberry jelly	(optional)
2 tablespoons orange juice	

1 Cut the ice cream into cubes and place in a basin.
2 Dissolve the jelly in a very little hot water and make up to a scant pint with cold water. Add the orange juice.
3 Pour, while still hot, over the ice cream. Stir briskly with a fork until well mixed.
4 Stir again and pour into the flan case. Leave in a cool place to set.
5 Decorate with strawberries, if available.

Orange apple flan

no cooking

you will need for 4 servings:

1 orange jelly	blanched almonds or
1 lb. cooking apples	thick cream for
4 oz. sugar	decorating
1 7-in. flan case (see page 87)	

1 Dissolve the jelly in a little hot water and make up to ½ pint with cold water.
2 Put the sugar and ¼ pint water in a pan. Bring to the boil.
3 Peel apples, cut into slices, removing the core.
4 Drop the apple slices into the syrup and simmer until tender.
5 Remove the apple slices to a measuring jug. Add enough of the syrup they were cooked in to make ½ pint in all. Mix with the jelly.
6 Spoon into flan case and leave until set.
7 Decorate with spikes of almond or cream.

Sunshine sundae

no cooking

you will need for 4 servings:

1 orange jelly	1 egg
1 small can pineapple cubes	1 dessertspoon sugar
	2 oz. glacé cherries

1 Dissolve the jelly in a little hot water. Make up to 1 pint with cold water and the juice from the fruit.
2 Divide half the jelly between 4 individual glasses. Leave in a cool place to set.
3 Separate the yolk and the white of the egg.
4 Blend the yolk with the sugar and pour on the remaining jelly (which should still be hot) stirring throughout. Leave until cool.
5 Place cherries and pineapple, saving some for decorating, on the jelly already set in the glasses.
6 Whisk the egg white until stiff. Fold into the cooled yolk mixture. Continue whisking until light and frothy.
7 Pile on top of fruit in the glasses. Leave until set.
8 Decorate with remaining fruit.

Strawberry and peach cream

no cooking

you will need for 4 servings:

1 strawberry jelly	2 level tablespoons sugar
3 tablespoons cornflour	$\frac{1}{2}$ oz. butter
$\frac{1}{2}$ pint milk	1 small can peaches

1 Dissolve jelly in a little hot water. Make up to 1 pint with cold water.
2 Pour into 1½-pint mould, rinsed out with cold water. Leave in a cool place to set.
3 Blend cornflour with a little of the milk, boil the remainder of the milk.
4 Pour the boiling milk on to the blended cornflour, stirring well.
5 Return to pan, bring to the boil and cook for 3 minutes.
6 Stir in sugar and butter.
7 Drain peaches, chop half of them and stir into the cornflour mixture, leave until cool.
8 Pour cornflour on to jelly. Leave until set.
9 Turn out and decorate with remaining peaches.

Raspberry mousse

no cooking

you will need for 4 servings:

1 raspberry jelly	1 small can raspberries
1 6-oz. can evaporated milk	macaroons or chopped nuts (optional)
2 teaspoons lemon juice	

1 Tie a double band of greaseproof paper round the outside of a 6-in. soufflé dish. (The paper should stand 2 inches above the rim of the dish.)
2 Dissolve the jelly in a little hot water, add the juice from the raspberries and cold water to make up to $\frac{3}{4}$ pint.
3 Leave in a cool place until the jelly is beginning to set.
4 Add the lemon juice to the milk (chilled if possible) and whisk until the milk is stiff enough to retain the mark of the whisk.
5 Whisk the jelly into the milk.
6 Press the raspberries (saving a few for decorating) through a sieve.
7 Fold the raspberry purée into the jelly mixture. Pour into the prepared soufflé case. Leave in a cold place to set.
8 Crush the macaroon if used.
9 Remove the paper from the soufflé. Press the crumbs or nuts, if used, round the sides of the mousse.
10 Decorate the top with the remaining raspberries.

Minute mousse

cooking time: 5 minutes

you will need for 4 servings:

1 packet chocolate flavoured cornflour	1 egg
4 level tablespoons castor sugar	1 pint milk

1 Mix the flavoured cornflour, sugar and egg yolk smoothly with a little of the cold milk.
2 Heat rest of the milk.
3 Pour on to the mixed cornflour, stirring well.
4 Return to saucepan and boil for 1 minute, stirring all the time, then cover the saucepan and allow to cool, but not set.
5 Whisk the egg white stiffly and lightly fold into the cooked mixture.
6 Pour into sundae glasses and decorate as liked.

Clementine pudding

no cooking

you will need for 4 servings:

1 lemon jelly	1 teaspoon cornflour
1 can mandarin	½ pint milk
oranges	1 tablespoon sugar
1 egg	

1 Dissolve the jelly in a little hot water.
2 Drain the fruit, adding the juice to the jelly.
3 Make the jelly and fruit juice up to ¾ pint with cold water. Leave in a cool place.
4 Beat the egg slightly, blend with the cornflour.
5 Heat the milk until almost boiling, stir on to the beaten egg.
6 Pour back into the pan, cook over a gentle heat until thick, stirring throughout.
7 Remove from the heat, stir in 1 tablespoon sugar. Leave until cool.
8 Chop half the fruit. Stir chopped fruit and jelly into the milk mixture.
9 Pour into a 1½-pint mould. Leave to set.
10 Turn out and decorate with remaining fruit.

Chocolate soufflé

cooking time: a few minutes to melt chocolate

you will need for 4 servings:

1 lemon jelly	1 oz. chocolate
4 oz. plain chocolate	buttons, optional
½ large can evaporated	thick cream, optional
milk	

1 Tie a double band of greaseproof paper round the outside of a 5–6 in. soufflé dish. The paper should come 2 inches above the rim of the dish.
2 Dissolve the jelly in ½ pint of hot water, leave to cool.
3 Place chocolate (broken into pieces) with 4 tablespoons water in a basin over a pan of hot water. Heat until chocolate is melted. Leave to cool.
4 Whisk the milk, chilled if possible, until thick.
5 Whisk the jelly, when almost setting, into the milk.
6 Fold in the melted chocolate, mix well.
7 Pour into prepared dish, leave in a cold place to set.
8 When set, remove paper, decorate top with chocolate buttons or whipped cream, as liked.

Simple lemon soufflé

no cooking

you will need for 4 servings:

1 lemon jelly	2 teaspoons lemon
1 6-oz. can evaporated	juice
milk	thick cream (optional)
	chocolate buttons

1 Prepare a small (6 in. diameter) soufflé dish by tying a band of paper round the outside of the dish. The paper should project 2 inches above the rim of the dish.
2 Dissolve the jelly in a little hot water, make up to ¾ pint with cold water. Leave in a cool place until almost setting.
3 Whisk the evaporated milk, chilled if possible, adding the lemon juice and continue whisking until thick and frothy.
4 Add jelly, gradually, whisking until mixed.
5 Pour into the prepared dish and leave in a cool place until set.
6 Remove paper carefully and decorate the edge with cream and chocolate buttons.

Mandarin jelly

no cooking

you will need for 4 servings:

small can mandarin	2 eggs
oranges	preserved ginger
1 orange jelly	(optional)

1 Drain mandarins, saving juice. Make juice up to ¾ pint with water.
2 Bring ¼ pint of this liquid to the boil, dissolve the jelly in it. Add the remaining cold liquid.
3 Separate eggs. Beat yolks with a fork, pour on the jelly whisking with a fork or whisk. Leave in a cold place until almost setting.
4 Chop mandarins, saving a few for decoration. Whisk egg whites until stiff.
5 Lightly fold mandarins and whites into jelly.
6 Pour into a mould and leave to set.
7 Turn out and decorate with remaining mandarin oranges and slices of preserved ginger.

Orange snow

no cooking

you will need for 4 servings:

1 orange jelly	2 tablespoons
2 eggs	desiccated coconut
3 oz. castor sugar	4 glacé cherries

1 Dissolve jelly in a little hot water. Make up to ¾ pint with cold water. *continued*

2 Separate yolks from whites of eggs.

3 Beat yolks with sugar until thick and creamy.

4 Gradually stir jelly into yolk mixture. Leave in a cold place until just beginning to set.

5 Whisk egg whites until stiff, fold into almost setting jelly.

6 Divide the mixture between 4 individual dishes.

7 Sprinkle with coconut and decorate each with a glacé cherry.

Summer pudding

cooking time: a few minutes to stew fruit

you will need for 4 servings:

1 strawberry jelly	2 tablespoons sugar
about 6 slices bread or plain cake	custard or thin cream
1 lb. mixed soft fruit (raspberries, redcurrants, etc.)	

1 Dissolve jelly in a little hot water, make up to $\frac{3}{4}$ pint with cold water.

2 Line the bottom and sides of a 1½-pint basin with bread or cake.

3 Spoon a little jelly over the bread or cake until it is all soaked.

4 Stew the fruit in $\frac{1}{4}$ pint water until tender, adding the sugar.

5 Stir the remaining jelly into the stewed fruit and leave until cold, but not set.

6 Pour into the prepared basin, cover the top with slices of bread or cake, pressing the top slices just into the jelly mixture.

7 Leave in a cool place until set.

8 Turn out and serve with custard or cream.

Strawberry honeycomb

cooking time: 10 minutes

you will need for 4 servings:

1 strawberry jelly	$\frac{1}{2}$ pint milk
2 eggs	biscuits

1 Dissolve the jelly in $\frac{1}{4}$ pint hot water.

2 Separate the yolks and whites of the eggs. Beat the yolks.

3 Warm the milk and pour on to the yolks, stirring.

4 Pour into a pan, previously rinsed in cold water, cook over a gentle heat until thick, stirring throughout.

5 Remove from heat and pour into a large bowl.

6 Stir the jelly into the milk mixture.

7 Whisk the whites until stiff, lightly fold into the jelly.

8 Pour into a 1½-pint mould and leave until set.

9 Turn out on to a plate and serve with crisp biscuits.

Strawberry cream

no cooking

you will need for 4 servings:

1 strawberry jelly	thick cream and strawberries, optional
about ½ pint milk	
1 egg	

1 Dissolve the jelly in $\frac{1}{4}$ pint hot water, leave to become cool.

2 Stir in enough milk to make up to 1 pint.

3 Separate yolk and white of egg.

4 Beat yolk lightly in a large basin, pour on the jelly mixture, stirring well.

5 Whisk the egg white until stiff, fold into the jelly.

6 Pour into a mould, previously rinsed out in cold water.

7 Leave in a cool place until set.

8 When set, turn out on to a plate. Decorate with thickened cream, and strawberries if available.

Raspberry caprice

no cooking

you will need for 4 servings:

5 oz. raspberries, canned or frozen	$\frac{1}{4}$ pint thick cream or custard
1 raspberry jelly	2 firm bananas

1 Drain canned fruit or thaw and drain frozen fruit.

2 Dissolve jelly in a little hot water, make up to $\frac{3}{4}$ pint with cold water and juice from fruit. Leave until cool and almost setting.

3 Whisk in the cream or custard.

4 Stir in the raspberries and bananas (sliced), saving some of each for decoration.

5 Pile into 4 individual dishes and leave to set.

6 Decorate with remaining fruit and serve at once.

Using lemon or orange juice: To prevent the banana slices used in decoration going brown, sprinkle with lemon or orange juice.

Raspberry chiffon

no cooking

you will need for 4 servings:

10 oz. packet frozen raspberries	¼ pint thick cream
1 raspberry jelly	2 egg whites
	sponge finger biscuits

1 Thaw raspberries according to the instructions on the packet. Strain well, saving the juice.
2 Bring juice to the boil, dissolve the jelly in it and make up to ¾ pint with cold water. Leave in a cool place until beginning to set.
3 Whisk the cream until thick.
4 Whisk the egg whites until stiff.
5 Fold the cream, egg whites and raspberries into the jelly, mix well together.
6 Pile into a glass bowl, leave to set.
7 Serve with sponge finger biscuits.

Raspberry condé

no cooking

you will need for 4 servings:

1 raspberry jelly	1 can creamed rice
1 can sliced peaches	

1 Dissolve the jelly in ¼ pint hot water, add the juice from the peaches made up to ½ pint with cold water. Leave in a cool place.
2 Chop half the peaches and stir into the rice.
3 Divide the rice between 4 individual dishes.
4 Arrange the whole peach slices on top of the rice.
5 Fill the dishes with the almost setting jelly. Leave until set.

Apricot dreams

cooking time: 15–20 minutes to cook apricots

you will need for 4 servings:

8 oz. dried apricots	2 eggs
3 oz. sugar	1 6-oz. can evaporated milk
1 lemon jelly	

1 Soak apricots overnight in enough water to cover.
2 Simmer in water until tender, add the sugar. Sieve or beat until smooth.
3 Dissolve jelly in a little hot water, stir into apricot purée. Make up to ¾ pint with water.
4 Separate eggs. Pour apricot mixture on to yolks, stirring well.
5 Whisk milk, chilled if possible, until thick.
6 Whisk whites until stiff.
7 Whisk whites and milk into jelly.
8 Taste, add more sugar if required.
9 Pile into 4 individual glasses, decorate with spikes of blanched almonds, if liked.

Mexican cream

cooking time: a few minutes to melt chocolate

you will need for 4 servings:

1 orange jelly	2 oz. plain chocolate
1 small can mandarin oranges, optional	1 6-oz. can evaporated milk

1 Dissolve the jelly in a little hot water, make up to ¾ pint with cold water (the juice from the fruit may also be used). Leave in a cool place until almost set.
2 Break the chocolate into pieces, place in a small basin over a pan of hot water. Heat gently until melted. Remove from heat.
3 Whisk the milk, previously chilled if possible, until thick.
4 Add the jelly, which should just be beginning to thicken, to the milk, whisking throughout.
5 Fold in the chocolate, stirring lightly, until well mixed.
6 Pour into a mould, previously rinsed with cold water.
7 When set, turn out on to a plate and decorate with mandarin oranges, if liked.

Pear Hélène

cooking time: 5 minutes

you will need for 4 servings:

1 tablespoon cornflour	½ teaspoon vanilla essence
½ pint water	1 family size block ice cream
2 oz. plain chocolate	
3 oz. castor sugar	4 halves canned pears
½ oz. butter	
pinch salt	

1 Blend the cornflour with a little of the cold water.
2 Put the rest of the water on to heat with the chocolate and sugar.
3 When the chocolate has melted, pour on to blended cornflour, return to the pan and boil for 3 minutes, stirring all the time.
4 Remove from heat and stir in the butter, salt and essence.
5 Cut block of ice cream into four slices. Arrange on individual dishes. Place a pear half, cut side down, on the ice cream.
6 Pour hot chocolate sauce over and serve.

Pear cream pudding

cooking time: 20 minutes

you will need for 4 servings:

1 lb. pears	1 packet chocolate
sugar	flavoured cornflour
cochineal (optional)	knob butter
¾ pint milk	walnuts (optional)

1 Prepare the pears and stew to pulp.
2 Sweeten to taste and, if liked, add a few drops colouring.
3 Mix the cornflour and 1–1½ oz. sugar with a little of the cold milk to a smooth paste.
4 Heat the remaining milk, add the blended cornflour and stir until boiling. Boil for 1 minute, stirring all the time.
5 Add the butter and pour the mixture into a pie dish. Top with the stewed pears and decorate with walnuts, if liked.
6 Serve hot.

With canned pears: To save time canned pears may be used. Heat gently in the juice from the can. Omit sugar.

St. Clement's chiffon pie

cooking time: 5 minutes

you will need for 4–6 servings:

8-in. pastry flan case	2 oz. castor sugar
1 can mandarin	2 egg yolks
oranges	juice 1 lemon
a little cold water	2 egg whites
1 oz. cornflour	

1 To make flan case, see page 87.
2 Drain the mandarins, and make the juice up to ½ pint with water.
3 Blend a little of the juice with the cornflour and the sugar and egg yolks and put the remaining juice on to heat.
4 When hot, pour on to the blended cornflour and return to the pan. Bring to the boil, stirring, and boil for 1 minute.
5 Add the lemon juice and the mandarins.
6 Whisk the egg whites until stiff. Lightly fold in the sauce mixture.
7 Pour into the cooked flan case and decorate with a few mandarin oranges.
8 Serve hot or cold.

Apple crumble

cooking time: 40 minutes

you will need for 4 servings:

1½ lb. apples	3 oz. butter or
about 4 tablespoons	margarine
water	6 oz. plain flour
4 oz. brown sugar	3 oz. castor sugar
little grated lemon	¼ teaspoon ground
rind	ginger

1 Peel, core and slice the apples into a pan. Add the water, brown sugar and grated lemon rind.
2 Cover and cook gently until the apples are soft.
3 When cooked, turn into a greased pie dish.
4 Rub the butter or margarine into the flour, add the sugar and ground ginger and mix well.
5 Sprinkle this mixture over the apple and press down lightly.
6 Cook in a moderate oven (350°F – Gas Mark 4), until golden brown.
7 When cooked, sprinkle with castor sugar and serve with cream or custard.

Apple dumplings

cooking time: 15 minutes

you will need for 4 servings:

1 lb. cooking apples	pinch mixed spice
½ pint water	3 oz. shredded suet
juice ½ lemon	1 teaspoon grated
2 oz. brown sugar	lemon rind
6 oz. self-raising flour	

1 Peel and slice the apples and place with the water, lemon juice and sugar in a saucepan. Bring to the boil.
2 Sieve the flour and spice, add the suet and lemon rind and mix to a stiff dough with water.
3 Shape the dough into 14 small balls.
4 When the apple mixture is boiling and the sugar has dissolved, drop in the dumplings, cover with a lid and allow to cook.

Castle puddings

cooking time: about 25 minutes

you will need for 4 servings:

4 oz. butter or	grated rind ½ lemon
margarine	4 oz. sieved plain flour
4 oz. castor sugar	1 level teaspoon
2 eggs	baking powder

1 Grease 6–7 dariole moulds.
2 Cream the butter or margarine with the sugar

until soft and white. Gradually beat in the eggs. Add the lemon rind.

3 Fold in the flour and baking powder.
4 Three-quarters fill each mould with the mixture and bake in a moderate oven (350°F – Gas Mark 4) until golden brown.
5 When cooked, turn out and serve with a jam sauce.

With vanilla: If liked, vanilla essence can be used instead of lemon rind.

These puddings can also be steamed. Cover with greased paper and steam for about 50 minutes. The mixture can also be cooked in a large basin.

Custard

cooking time: about 10 minutes

you will need for 4 servings:

3 level tablespoons custard powder	2 rounded tablespoons sugar
1 pint milk	

1 Blend the custard powder with a little of the milk.
2 Bring the remaining milk to the boil.
3 Pour on to the blended custard, stirring all the time.
4 Rinse the pan with cold water, return the custard to the pan and bring to the boil over a gentle heat, stirring all the time.
5 Boil for 2–3 minutes, add the sugar.
6 If cold custard is required, cover with a plate to prevent a skin forming.

Fruit trifle

no cooking

you will need for 4 servings:

3–4 slices stale cake	1 small can fruit salad
2 tablespoons raspberry jam	1 pint thick custard

1 Spread cake with jam and cut into cubes, place in a glass bowl.
2 Drain juice from fruit and sprinkle over the cake. Arrange fruit, chopped if preferred, on the cake.
3 Pour cool custard over and leave until cold.

Mandarin trifle: Make as above, using chocolate cake and mandarin oranges instead of fruit salad.

Gooseberry fool

cooking time: about 20 minutes

you will need for 4 servings:

1½ lb. gooseberries	8 oz. sugar
3 tablespoons water	½ pint thick custard

1 Top and tail the goosberries and cook in the water.
2 When nearly tender, add the sugar.
3 When soft, pass through a sieve and allow to become cold.
4 Slightly whip the custard and fold into the gooseberry purée.
5 Pour into a glass dish and serve very cold.

Jellied fruit flan

cooking time: about 10 minutes

you will need for 4 servings:

1 cooked pastry flan case (see page 87)	2 teaspoons powdered gelatine
canned fruit	sugar to taste

1 Fill the flan case with drained, canned fruit.
2 Heat ¼ pint of the drained juice in a small pan and stir in the gelatine.
3 Heat gently until the gelatine dissolves, add sugar to taste.
4 Leave in a cool place until just about to set.
5 Spoon over the fruit and leave until set.

Cranberry lattice tart

cooking time: 25 minutes

you will need for 4 servings:

4 oz. plain flour	1 teaspoon castor sugar
2 oz. cornflour	
3 oz. butter	1 egg yolk
For the filling:	
2 oz. raisins	1 oz. walnuts, chopped
2 oz. currants	
2 oz. sultanas	8 oz. can cranberry sauce
1 oz. mixed peel, chopped	

1 Sieve together the flour and cornflour.
2 Rub in the butter until the mixture resembles fine breadcrumbs. Add the sugar and egg yolk and mix to a stiff dough.
3 Roll out, line a 7-in. flan ring.
4 Mix all the ingredients for the filling together and place in the flan case. Make a lattice design on the top of the tart using the pastry trimming.
5 Bake at 350°F, Gas Mark 4 for 20–25 minutes.
6 Serve hot or cold with cream or custard.

Pancakes

cooking time: about 6 minutes each pancake

you will need for 4 servings:

8 oz. plain flour	melted cooking fat or
¼ teaspoon salt	oil
2 eggs	lemon
1 pint milk	castor sugar

1 Sieve the flour and salt into a mixing bowl. Make a well in the centre and break the eggs into this.
2 Add about ¼ pint of the milk and stir, gradually working in the flour from the sides.
3 Add enough milk to give a stiff batter consistency. Beat thoroughly for at least 5 minutes, then cover, and leave to stand for 30 minutes.
4 Add the remaining milk and stir well. Pour the mixture into a jug.
5 Pour about 1 tablespoon of melted fat or butter into a small clean frying pan or omelette pan.
6 Just as the fat is beginning to smoke, pour in enough batter to cover the bottom of the pan thinly. Tilt the pan to ensure the batter runs over evenly.
7 Move the frying pan gently over a quick heat until the pancake is set and brown underneath. Make sure it is loose at the side and turn it over with a fish slice or a broad-bladed knife.
8 Brown on the other side and turn on to a sugared sheet of greaseproof paper. Sprinkle with sugar and lemon juice and roll up. Keep hot while cooking the rest.
9 Serve the pancakes sprinkled with castor sugar and accompanied by wedges of lemon.

Jam pancakes: Make the pancakes as for plain pancakes and spread with the jam before rolling up.

Ice cream

This is easily made at home from prepared ice cream mix using the instructions on the can.

Cakes and Biscuits

No matter how busy you are, there are still times when you may feel the urge to become an old-fashioned cook, and to produce home baked cakes, fragrant and fresh, from your own oven.

The following recipes have been especially designed to meet the limited schedules of even the busiest modern cooks, without any sacrifice of quality.

Scones

cooking time: small scones 7–10 minutes, scone round 10–15 minutes

you will need:

8 oz. flour	1 oz. sugar
2 teaspoons baking powder	¼ pint milk
¼ teaspoon salt	beaten egg or milk for glazing
2 oz. fat (butter, margarine or lard)	

1 Grease and flour a baking tray.
2 Sieve flour, baking powder and salt.
3 Rub the fat into the flour with the finger tips.
4 Add the sugar and any other ingredients to be used (see following recipes).
5 Stir in the milk and mix quickly to a soft dough.
6 Turn on to a floured board. Flour hands and form dough into a ball. Cut into two pieces.
7 Press each lightly by hand, or roll into a round, ¾ in. thick.
8 Cut out with 2-in. cutter or divide each round into quarters with a sharp knife. Do not cut through.
9 Place on a baking tray, brush with beaten egg or milk.
10 Bake in a hot oven (425°F – Gas Mark 7).
11 Cool on a wire tray.
12 Serve hot or cold.

Breakfast scones: Use basic recipe with or without the sugar. Serve buttered, with cherry jam or marmalade.

Brown scones: Make as for basic recipe, using half wholemeal and half white flour.

Cheese scones: Make as for basic recipe, omitting the sugar and adding 4 oz. grated cheese and a pinch of dry mustard.

Fancy scones: Make as for basic recipe, adding 1 oz. chopped mixed peel and 1 oz. chopped glacé cherries.

Fruit scones: Make as for basic recipe, adding 2 oz. currants, sultanas or raisins.

Ginger scones: Make as for basic recipe, omitting baking powder. Add ½ teaspoon bicarbonate of soda, ½ teaspoon powdered ginger and 1–2 tablespoons syrup or treacle.

Oatmeal scones: Make as for basic recipe, using 4 oz. flour and 4 oz. fine oatmeal.

Potato scones: Make as for basic recipe, using 4 oz. flour and 4 oz. cooked, sieved potato.

Soda scones: Make as for basic recipe, omitting baking powder. Add 1 teaspoon cream of tartar and ½ teaspoon bicarbonate of soda.

Sour milk scones: Make as for basic recipe, omitting baking powder. Add ½ teaspoon bicarbonate of soda, ½ teaspoon cream of tartar and mix with ¼ pint of sour milk.

Tea scones: Add 1 beaten egg to the basic recipe and use a little less milk. Serve hot with butter or cream and strawberry or raspberry jam.

Treacle scones: Make as ginger scones, omitting ginger and adding ½ teaspoon mixed spice.

Girdle scones: Use basic recipe. Divide each large piece of dough into eight sections. Heat a girdle, the hot plate of an electric cooker, the girdle sheet of a cooker or a frying pan until moderately hot. Grease well. Cook scones for 4–5 minutes on each side. Serve hot.

Drop scones

cooking time: about 4 minutes each
you will need:

8 oz. self-raising flour	pinch salt
3 level teaspoons baking powder *or*	3 level teaspoons cinnamon or mixed spice
8 oz. plain flour	2 oz. castor sugar
3 well-rounded teaspoons baking powder *or*	1 egg
8 oz. plain flour	¼ pint and 5 tablespoons milk
1 level teaspoon bicarbonate of soda	1 oz. melted margarine
2 level teaspoons cream of tartar	additional melted margarine butter

1 Have ready a girdle or strong frying pan (or the hot plate of an electric cooker). Brush with melted margarine and place over a moderate heat.
2 Sieve the flour, baking powder (or other raising agent), salt, cinnamon or spice together twice into a bowl.
3 Beat the egg with the milk and gradually add to the dry ingredients.
4 Drop dessertspoons of the batter on to the hot girdle, well apart.
5 Continue until all the batter is used, keeping the cooked scones hot under a clean tea towel.
6 Serve at once, spread with butter.

Savoury drop scones: Make as for drop scones, replacing the sugared spices with 4 heaped tablespoons grated cheese or 2 rounded teaspoons Parmesan cheese, a pinch of cayenne pepper and a little extra salt, if liked.

Small plain cakes

cooking time: 15–20 minutes
you will need:

8 oz. plain flour	4 oz. sugar
2 teaspoons baking powder	3–4 oz. fruit, optional
½ teaspoon salt	2 eggs
4 oz. margarine	milk to mix

1 Grease patty tins or small paper cases.
2 Sieve flour, salt and baking powder and spice if used.
3 Rub in fat with tips of fingers until mixture looks like breadcrumbs.
4 Add sugar, and fruit if used.
5 Beat the eggs and stir into the mixture, adding a little milk if necessary to mix to a dropping consistency.
6 Bake in a moderately hot oven (400°F – Gas Mark 6) for 5 minutes. Reduce heat to moderate (350°F – Gas Mark 4) and continue cooking until well risen and golden.

Cherry cakes: Make as above, adding 2 oz. glacé cherries, ½ teaspoon vanilla essence.

Chocolate cakes: Make as above, replacing 1 tablespoon flour with 1 tablespoon cocoa and adding ½ teaspoon vanilla essence.

Coconut buns: Make as before, adding 2 tablespoons coconut and $\frac{1}{2}$ teaspoon vanilla essence.

Coffee buns: Make as before, adding 2 tablespoons coffee essence and 2 oz. currants.

Cinnamon buns: Make as before, adding $\frac{1}{2}$ teaspoon cinnamon and $\frac{1}{2}$ teaspoon grated lemon rind.

Ginger cakes: Make as before, adding 2 oz. chopped ginger and $\frac{1}{2}$ teaspoon ground ginger.

Rice buns: Replace 2 oz. flour with 2 oz. ground rice.

Fruit buns: Make as before, adding 3–4 oz. raisins, currants or sultanas, 1 oz. chopped peel and $\frac{1}{4}$ teaspoon nutmeg.

Treacle buns: Make as before, adding 1 tablespoon treacle, omit baking powder, and use $\frac{1}{2}$ teaspoon bicarbonate of soda.

To steam: Any of these mixtures may be steamed in a greased basin or individual moulds. Serve as a pudding with jam or custard sauce.

Coconut rockies

cooking time: 10–12 minutes

you will need:

5 oz. self-raising flour	1 small egg
pinch salt	3 oz. desiccated
4 oz. margarine	coconut
4 oz. sugar	

1 Sieve the flour and salt.
2 Cream the fat and sugar and beat in the egg.
3 Stir in the flour and coconut.
4 Half-fill small paper cases with the mixture.
5 Place on a baking sheet and bake in a hot oven (425°F – Gas Mark 7).
6 Cool on a wire tray.

Almond twists

cooking time: 10 minutes

you will need:

5 oz. plain flour	1 egg
pinch salt	few drops almond
3 oz. butter	essence
2 dessertspoons	
castor sugar	
For the topping:	
little beaten egg white	chopped almonds,
castor sugar	optional

1 Sift flour with salt. Rub fat in lightly. Add the sugar.
2 Stir in beaten egg and essence. Mix to a soft dough.
3 Divide dough into 9 equal portions, roll each into a long 'sausage' about 7 in. long on a lightly floured surface.
4 Curl each round into a 'pincurl' shape. Place on a baking sheet.
5 Brush the top of each with egg white and sprinkle with castor sugar and finely chopped blanched almonds, if available.
6 Bake in a moderately hot oven (400°F – Gas Mark 6) until golden.
7 Leave to cool on a wire tray.

Lemon fingers

cooking time: 20–25 minutes

you will need:

4 oz. luxury	5 oz. plain flour
margarine	lemon curd
2 oz. castor sugar	

1 Place the margarine and sugar in a bowl.
2 Sieve the flour into the fat and sugar.
3 Beat all together until soft and creamy with a wooden spoon – about 2 minutes.
4 Spread mixture into a Swiss roll tin. Mark in lines across surface using the back of a fork.
5 Bake near the top of a moderate oven (350°F – Gas Mark 4).
6 While hot cut into fingers and lift carefully on to a wire tray with a palette knife.
7 When cold sandwich together with lemon curd and dust with icing sugar.

Queen cakes

cooking time: 20 minutes

you will need:

6 oz. self-raising flour	4 oz. castor sugar
good pinch salt	2 eggs
4 oz. butter or	milk to mix
margarine	4 oz. currants

1 Sieve the flour and salt into a bowl.
2 Cream the fat and sugar until light in colour and fluffy in texture.
3 Beat the eggs lightly with a fork.
4 Beat into the creamed fat, folding in a little flour.
5 Stir in the milk.

6 Fold in the remaining flour using a metal spoon, and stir in the fruit.

7 Half fill paper baking cases (about 20) on a baking sheet, or greased patty tins.

8 Bake on the middle shelf of a moderately hot oven (375°F – Gas Mark 5).

With vanilla, lemon or orange: The flavour may be varied by adding 2–3 drops of vanilla essence, or grated lemon rind or orange rind to the creamed fat.

Ginger nuts

cooking time: 15–20 minutes

you will need:

4 oz. self-raising flour	½ teaspoon bicarbonate soda
2 level teaspoons ground ginger	2 oz. white vegetable fat
1 level teaspoon ground cinnamon	2 tablespoons golden syrup
1 level dessertspoon sugar	

1 Sieve the dry ingredients.

2 Melt the fat and syrup over a low heat and allow to cool.

3 Stir in the dry ingredients, mixing well with a wooden spoon.

4 Take pieces, about the size of a walnut, and roll into a ball between the palms of the hands.

5 Place well apart on a greased baking tray. Flatten slightly.

6 Bake in a moderate oven (375°F – Gas Mark 5).

Almond drops: Make as before, omitting spices but adding ½ teaspoon almond essence with the syrup mixture. Press half a blanched almond into the centre of each ball before baking.

Flapjacks

cooking time: 30–35 minutes

you will need:

3 oz. margarine	4 oz. golden syrup
2 oz. demerara sugar	8 oz. rolled oats

1 Melt the margarine, sugar and syrup together in a pan.

2 Add the rolled oats and mix together thoroughly.

3 Turn the mixture into a greased tin, 11½ × 7½ inches.

4 Spread over the tin evenly and press down firmly.

5 Bake on the middle shelf of a moderate oven (350°F – Gas Mark 4).

6 Remove from the oven.

7 Cut into 16 pieces and leave to cool in the tin.

Teatime biscuits

cooking time: 15–20 minutes

you will need:

8 oz. self-raising flour	grated rind ½ lemon
3 oz. butter	approximately 1 tablespoon water
3 oz. sugar	
1 egg yolk	

1 Sieve the flour.

2 Cream the fat and sugar, beat in the lemon rind and egg yolk.

3 Work in the flour, adding enough water to make a soft dough.

4 Roll out on a lightly floured surface about ⅛ in. thick.

5 Cut into rounds or fancy shapes with cutters.

6 Bake in a moderately hot oven (375°F – Gas Mark 5).

7 Lift carefully on to a wire tray with a palette knife. Leave until cold and crisp.

8 Dredge with castor sugar.

Flaky hot biscuits

cooking time: 10–15 minutes

you will need:

7 oz. self-raising flour	2 oz. cooking fat
1 teaspoon baking powder	¼ pint milk (short measure)
½ teaspoon salt	

1 Sieve the flour, baking powder and salt together.

2 Cut the fat into pieces about ¼ in. in size and stir into the dry ingredients.

3 Make a well in the centre and pour in the milk.

4 Stir with a knife and then knead lightly on a floured surface for about 1 minute.

5 Roll out to ⅓ in. thickness.

6 Cut out with a floured cutter and place on a greased baking tray so that they are touching one another.

7 Bake in a hot oven (425°F – Gas Mark 7).

8 Serve hot with butter.

Viennese shortcakes

cooking time: 20 minutes

you will need:

4 oz. self-raising flour	½ teaspoon vanilla
4 oz. plain flour	essence
7 oz. butter	butter cream (see
2 oz. icing sugar	page 85)

1 Grease 2 baking sheets.
2 Sieve both the flours together in a bowl.
3 Cream fat and sugar adding the vanilla essence.
4 Beat in the flour working the mixture with a wooden spoon until smooth.
5 Put mixture into a forcing bag filled with a large rose pipe.
6 Pipe mixture in circles or strips on to the trays.
7 Bake in a moderately hot oven (375°F – Gas Mark 5).
8 Cool on a wire tray. When cold, sandwich with butter cream.

Viennese fingers: Make recipe above, piping the mixture in strips about 2½ in. long. Sandwich the biscuits with butter cream and dip the ends in melted chocolate.

Viennese tartlets: Cut out rounds of plain biscuit mixture. Using a small pipe, pipe Viennese shortcake mixture in a circle around the edge of each biscuit round. Bake in a moderately hot oven (375°F – Gas Mark 5) for 25–30 minutes. Fill the centre of each tartlet, when cold, with lemon curd or raspberry jam. Dust with icing sugar.

Sponge fingers

cooking time: 7–10 minutes

you will need:

2 oz. flour	2 oz. castor sugar
2 eggs	castor sugar to dredge

1 Grease and flour a tray of sponge finger tins.
2 Sieve the flour.
3 Whisk the eggs and sugar together in a basin over hot water until thick.
4 Fold in the flour.
5 Turn mixture into the tins, sprinkle well with castor sugar.
6 Bake in a hot oven (425°F – Gas Mark 7) until golden and firm.
7 Turn out on to a wire tray to cool.

Lemon sponge fingers: Make as before and when cold sandwich biscuits together in pairs with lemon curd. Dip ends of each in lemon flavoured glacé icing (see page 85).

Danish delights: Make sponge fingers as before. Spread thick glacé icing (see page 85) over top of each biscuit and sprinkle thickly with chopped mixed peel.

Chocolate fingers: Make sponge fingers, see left. Melt a 2-oz. bar plain chocolate in a cup. Dip each finger into the chocolate, allowing the chocolate to come half-way up each finger. Stand the biscuits in a small cup or basin, plain side down, until dry.

Sponge drops: Make mixture as for sponge fingers, see left, adding a few drops vanilla essence to whisked eggs and sugar. Spoon the mixture into a forcing bag, fitted with a plain ½-in. nozzle. Pipe into rounds, well apart, on a greased floured tin. Bake in a hot oven (425°F – Gas Mark 7) for 7–10 minutes until lightly coloured. Lift carefully on to a wire tray. When cold, dredge with castor sugar or coat top of each with a little glacé icing (see page 85).

Scotch shortbread 1

cooking time: 30–40 minutes

you will need:

6 oz. plain flour	2 oz. castor sugar
2 oz. cornflour	½ yolk 1 egg
4 oz. butter	

1 Sieve the flour and cornflour into a bowl.
2 Rub in the butter, add the sugar.
3 Stir in the egg yolk and work all well together.
4 Turn mixture on to a floured surface and knead well, until mixture is smooth and free from cracks.
5 Shape mixture into a round cake.
6 Mark all round the edge with back of a fork. Prick the centre lightly with a fork.
7 Bake in a slow oven (335°F – Gas Mark 3).
8 Lift carefully on to a wire tray.
9 Sprinkle with castor sugar and leave until cool.

Shortbread fingers or crescents (*illustrated on cover*): Make mixture as before. Roll out into an oblong. Cut into fingers or crescents and prick down the centre of each. Place on a **baking**

tray and bake for 15–20 minutes at 350°F –
Gas Mark 4. Cool on a wire tray and sprinkle
with castor sugar.

Scotch shortbread 2

cooking time: about 45 minutes

you will need:

8 oz. butter	12 oz. plain flour
4 oz. castor sugar	4 oz. cornflour

1 Cream the butter and sugar together very
thoroughly.
2 Sift together the flour and cornflour and
gradually work into the butter mixture.
3 Knead the shortbread into a round shape on
a baking tray and crimp the edges between
the thumb and forefinger: or the mixture may
be pressed firmly into a flat tin 7×11 in.
4 Prick well and bake in a slow oven (335°F –
Gas Mark 3).
5 When cooked, cut into wedges or fingers and
dredge with castor sugar.

Abernethy biscuits

cooking time: about 10 minutes

you will need:

6 oz. plain flour	1 level teaspoon
2 oz. cornflour	caraway seeds or
1 level teaspoon	ground caraway
baking powder	1 egg
3 oz. butter	about 1 tablespoon
3 oz. sugar	milk

1 Sift flour, baking powder and cornflour together.
2 Rub in the butter. Add sugar and caraway seeds.
3 Mix to a firm dough with the beaten egg and
milk.
4 Roll out, cut into rounds.
5 Bake in a moderate oven (350°F – Gas Mark
4).

Lemon coconut cookies

cooking time: 8–10 minutes

you will need:

4 oz. plain flour	½ teaspoon vanilla
pinch salt	essence
4 oz. butter or	lemon cream or curd
margarine	coconut
1 oz. icing sugar	

1 Sieve flour and salt.
2 Cream fat and sugar, adding essence.

3 Stir in flour and mix well.
4 Take one level dessertspoon dough for each
cookie and form into a ball, flatten slightly.
5 Place the cookies 1 in. apart on an ungreased
baking tray.
6 Bake in a moderately hot oven (400°F – Gas
Mark 6) until lightly browned.
7 Cool on a wire tray.
8 Spread lemon cream (see below) or curd on
each cookie.
9 Sprinkle with desiccated coconut.

Chocolate orange cookies: Make as above. Top
the cookies with orange flavoured glacé icing,
see page 85, and sprinkle with grated chocolate.
Leave in a cool place until dry.

Almond cookies: Make as above, replacing
vanilla with almond essence. Press half a
blanched almond in the centre of each cookie
before baking.

Favourite cookies: Make as before, replacing
vanilla with lemon essence. Coat cookies with
thick white glacé icing (see page 85) and place
half a glacé cherry in the centre of each. Leave in
a cool place to dry.

Lemon cream

cooking time: 10–15 minutes

you will need:

1 egg	3 tablespoons lemon
rind 1 lemon, finely	juice
grated	1 oz. butter
6 oz. castor sugar	

1 Beat the egg slightly in a basin over a small
pan of hot water.
2 Add the lemon rind, sugar, lemon juice and
butter.
3 Stir and cook over hot water until well blended
and thick. Allow to cool.

Swiss roll

cooking time: 7–9 minutes

you will need:

4 oz. flour	1 tablespoon hot water
3 eggs	warmed jam
4 oz. castor sugar	castor sugar

1 Grease a Swiss roll tin (9×13 in.) and line
with greased greaseproof paper, cut 2 inches
larger all round than the tin. *continued*

2 Sieve the flour.

3 Whisk the eggs and sugar in a large bowl over a pan of hot water. Continue whisking until the mixture is thick and fluffy and stiff enough to hold the impression of the whisk for a few seconds. Remove from over water.

4 Stir in the water and lightly fold in the flour.

5 Put the mixture into the prepared tin, tilting the tin so that the mixture is spread evenly.

6 Bake in a hot oven (425°F – Gas Mark 7) until golden and springy to touch.

7 Spread a sheet of greaseproof or a damp clean tea towel with castor sugar. Turn the sponge out on to this and remove the paper.

8 Using a sharp knife, trim all the crisp outer edges, keeping the shape as neat as possible.

9 Quickly spread the surface of the cake with warmed jam to within ½-in. of the edge.

10 Make a long cut half-way through the depth of the sponge, 1 in. from the near edge of the sponge. Roll up the sponge as tightly as possible, using the paper or cloth to help keep the roll in shape.

11 Cool on a wire tray and sprinkle with castor sugar.

Victoria sandwich

cooking time: 25 minutes

you will need:

4 oz. butter or margarine	4 oz. self-raising flour
4 oz. sugar	water or milk, about 1 tablespoon (optional)
2 eggs*	jam

* If large eggs are used, additional liquid is not necessary, but water or milk may be added with the egg to give a soft dropping consistency.

** For 8-in. sandwich tins you will need: 3 eggs and 6 oz. fat, sugar and self-raising flour. Bake for 30–35 minutes.

1 Grease two 7-in. sandwich tins** and dust with flour.

2 Cream the fat and sugar.

3 Beat in the eggs gradually.

4 Fold in the sieved flour.

5 Divide between the two tins, making sure the mixture is level.

6 Bake on the top shelf of a moderately hot oven (375°F – Gas Mark 5).

7 Turn out on to a wire rack to cool.

8 When cold, sandwich together with jam and dust the top with sugar.

Raspberry gâteau

no cooking

you will need:

8 oz. raspberries	¼ pint thick cream
2 oz. castor sugar	thick white glacé icing, lemon flavoured (see page 85)
2 8-in. rounds of sandwich or sponge cake	

1 Mash half the raspberries with the castor sugar.

2 Spread over one cake, top with cream, whisked until thick, and cover with the second round of cake.

3 Coat with thick glacé icing and decorate with remaining raspberries.

4 Serve as soon as the icing is set.

Mandarin gâteau: Make as before, using drained mandarin oranges in place of the raspberries and omitting the castor sugar. Sprinkle the icing with coarsely grated chocolate and decorate with mandarins.

Strawberry meringue gâteau: Make as before, using strawberries instead of raspberries, piling more whipped cream with the strawberries on top of the cake. Decorate with small whole meringues or pieces of meringue.

Peach gâteau: Make as before, using drained peaches in place of raspberries and omitting the castor sugar. Sprinkle the icing with chopped, toasted almonds.

Chocolate cake

cooking time: about 25 minutes

you will need:

4 oz. luxury margarine	2 eggs
5 oz. castor sugar	1 tablespoon milk
4 oz. self-raising flour	glacé icing (see page 85) or
1 heaped tablespoon cocoa	castor sugar

For the filling:

2 oz. plain chocolate	1 dessertspoon milk
2 oz. luxury margarine	flavouring essence (optional)
1 oz. castor sugar	
2 dessertspoons hot water	

1 Grease two 7-in. sandwich tins and line the bottom with greaseproof paper.
2 Put margarine and sugar in a mixing bowl. Sieve in flour and cocoa.
3 Add milk and eggs and beat all ingredients together with a wooden spoon for 2 minutes.
4 Divide the mixture between the tins and smooth the top.
5 Bake in the middle of a moderate oven (350°F – Gas Mark 4) for 20–25 minutes.
6 Turn on to a wire tray to cool. When the cakes are cold, sandwich together with the filling and coat the top with glacé icing or sprinkle with castor sugar.

To make the filling

1 Melt the chocolate in a basin over hot water.
2 Allow the chocolate to cool and whisk it together with the margarine and sugar until light and fluffy.
3 Add the water, milk and 1–2 drops flavouring.
4 Whisk again and use.
For a 'special' cake, make double the quantity of filling and use half of it as a frosty topping using small palette knife or fork to swirl a design on the top before the filling sets.

To make chocolate icing

Add a few drops water and olive oil to melted chocolate. Or, make a coating icing: blend 2 oz. melted chocolate with 4 oz. icing sugar and 1 tablespoon water. A few drops of oil can be added for extra gloss.

Quick mix cakes for the unexpected guest

These 'minute-mix' cakes are made in one stage. No creaming is required. Their success depends on the use of a quick creaming fat, so choose luxury or superfine margarine.

Orange layer cake

cooking time: 20 minutes

you will need:

8 oz. self-raising flour	3 eggs
pinch salt	rind 1 orange, finely
1 level teaspoon	grated
baking powder	about 3 tablespoons
6 oz. castor sugar	milk
6 oz. luxury margarine	

Lemon layer cake: Use the same ingredients as for orange layer cake, using lemon rind instead of orange rind.

Chocolate cake

cooking time: 20 minutes

you will need:

6 oz. self-raising flour	6 oz. luxury
pinch salt	margarine
4 level tablespoons	3 eggs
cocoa	$\frac{1}{4}$ teaspoon vanilla
small pinch	essence
bicarbonate soda	about 3 tablespoons
6 oz. castor sugar	milk

Coconut cake

cooking time: 20 minutes

you will need:

6 oz. self-raising flour	$\frac{1}{4}$ teaspoon vanilla
pinch salt	essence
1 level teaspoon	2 oz. desiccated
baking powder	coconut
6 oz. castor sugar	about 4 tablespoons
6 oz. luxury margarine	milk
3 eggs	

Method of making quick mix cakes

1 Grease two 8-in. sandwich tins and line the bottom of each with a round of greaseproof paper.
2 Chop up the margarine in a mixing bowl.
3 Sieve in the dry ingredients.
4 Add the sugar, eggs, essence or flavouring and the milk.
5 Beat well for 1 minute until evenly mixed, adding another spoonful of milk if necessary to make a dropping consistency.
6 Spread the mixture into the two tins.
7 Bake in a moderately hot oven (375°F – Gas Mark 5) on the third shelf from the top until firm, then turn on to a wire tray to cool.
8 When cold, sandwich together with butter cream, see page 85, and ice and decorate as liked.

One-stage cake

cooking time: 25–35 minutes

you will need:

4 oz. self-raising flour	4 oz. luxury margarine
1 level teaspoon baking powder	2 eggs
4 oz. sugar	filling and icing as liked

1 Grease two 7-in. sandwich tins and line the bottom of each with a round of greaseproof paper.
2 Sieve the flour and baking powder into a bowl.
3 Put the margarine and sugar into the bowl.
4 Break the eggs into the bowl. Mix all the ingredients together with a wooden spoon – this should take about 1 minute.
5 Divide the mixture between the tins. Bake in a slow oven (335°F – Gas Mark 3) on the middle shelf.
6 When the cakes are cold, sandwich together with filling and coat the top with icing.

Note:

If liked, the cake may be baked in one 8-in. cake tin, greased and the bottom lined with greaseproof paper. Cook for 35–45 minutes.

Party time cake

cooking time: 12–15 minutes

you will need:

3 eggs	6 oz. self-raising flour
1½ tablespoons milk	1½ teaspoons baking powder
½ teaspoon vanilla essence	3 oz. butter, melted
6 oz. castor sugar	

For the filling:

3 oz. butter	1 dessertspoon hot water
6 oz. icing sugar, sieved	glacé icing (see page 85)
3 tablespoons lemon curd	

1 Whisk the egg, milk and essence together in a bowl.
2 Gradually add the sugar.
3 Fold in the flour, sieved with the baking powder.
4 Stir in the melted butter lightly, making sure it is well blended in.
5 Divide the mixture between two well-greased 7-in. sandwich tins.
6 Bake in a moderately hot oven (375°F – Gas Mark 5). Cool in the tins for 5 minutes before turning out.

7 Make the filling. Cream the butter and sugar then add the lemon curd and hot water. Beat until smooth.
8 Sandwich the cakes together, when cold, with the filling and coat the cake with glacé icing.

Golden cakes

cooking time: 15–20 minutes

you will need:

8 oz. flour	4 oz. sugar
½ teaspoon baking powder	3 eggs
pinch salt	3 tablespoons marmalade
4 oz. margarine	lemon icing

1 Grease eighteen queen cake or deep patty tins.
2 Sieve flour, baking powder and salt.
3 Cream fat and sugar.
4 Beat in the eggs one at a time, beating each in well before adding the next.
5 Stir in the marmalade. Fold in the dry ingredients.
6 Half fill prepared tins. Bake at 375°F – Gas Mark 5.
7 Cool on a wire tray. Top each with lemon glacé icing (see page 85).

Cherry cake

cooking time: about 1½ hours

you will need:

8 oz. self-raising flour	3 eggs
2 oz. fine semolina	3 tablespoons milk
6 oz. butter or margarine	3 oz. sliced glacé cherries
6 oz. castor sugar	

1 Well grease a 7-in. cake tin or small loaf tin.
2 Sift the flour and semolina twice.
3 Soften the butter, gradually add the sugar, beating until light and fluffy.
4 Whisk the eggs and add gradually, beating well and adding two spoonfuls of the sifted flour mixture after adding about half the eggs.
5 Stir in the remainder of the flour and semolina and the milk.
6 Stir in the cherries, reserving a few for the top of the cake.
7 Turn the mixture into the prepared tin, arrange remaining cherries on top and bake in a moderate oven (350°F – Gas Mark 4).

Dundee cake

cooking time: 2½–3 hours

you will need:

6 tablespoons corn oil	6 oz. sultanas
2 eggs	4 oz. peel
6 oz. soft brown sugar	2 oz. glacé cherries, chopped
10 oz. plain flour	2 oz. almonds, blanched and chopped
pinch salt	
1½ level teaspoons baking powder	2 oz. almonds, blanched (for top of cake)
2 tablespoons milk	
6 oz. currants	

1 Grease and line a 2-lb. cake tin. Prepare the fruit and dredge with a little of the flour.
2 Beat the corn oil, eggs and sugar together well, then add the flour, sifted with salt and baking powder. Add the milk and finally stir in the fruit and nuts.
3 Turn into the prepared tin and bake in a slow oven (310°F – Gas Mark 2).
4 After the first 30 minutes arrange the remaining almonds on top of the cake.

Fruit loaf

cooking time: 45 minutes

you will need:

12 oz. self-raising flour	1 tablespoon syrup
1 teaspoon baking powder	1 tablespoon black treacle
2 oz. sugar	¼ pint and 4 tablespoons milk
4 oz. dried fruit	

1 Sieve the dry ingredients together in a bowl.
2 Add the dried fruit.
3 Melt the syrup and treacle in the milk and stir into the dry ingredients.
4 Pour into a greased 1-lb. loaf tin and bake in a moderate oven (350°F – Gas Mark 4).
5 Serve sliced, spread with butter.

Gingerbread

cooking time: about 1¼ hours

you will need:

10 oz. plain flour	3 oz. chopped candied peel
2 oz. cornflour	
1 level teaspoon bicarbonate soda	2 oz. chopped crystallized ginger
1 level teaspoon mixed spice	8 oz. treacle
	¼ pint milk
2 level teaspoons ground ginger	6 tablespoons corn oil
4 oz. soft brown sugar	1 beaten egg

1 Prepare a $10 \times 7 \times 2$-in. tin, greasing lightly.
2 Sift flour, cornflour, bicarbonate soda and spices together into a mixing bowl.
3 Stir in the sugar, peel and crystallized ginger.
4 Warm treacle, add milk, oil and egg.
5 Pour all at once into the sifted dry ingredients and beat well together.
6 Pour into the prepared tin and bake about 1¼ hours in a moderate oven (350°F – Gas Mark 4).

Truffle cakes

you will need:

4 oz. stale sponge cake	chocolate glacé icing (see page 85) or melted chocolate
4 oz. castor sugar	chocolate vermicelli
4 oz. ground almonds	
apricot jam	
almond or rum essence (optional)	

1 Grate the cake into crumbs or rub through a coarse sieve into a mixing bowl.
2 Add the sugar and almonds.
3 Warm the jam over a gentle heat and sieve.
4 Blend the cake and almond mixture to a firm paste with the jam, adding a few drops almond or rum essence if liked.
5 Shape the mixture into 12–18 balls and leave in a cool place until firm.
6 Dip each ball in glacé icing or melted chocolate, using a skewer.
7 Roll in chocolate vermicelli and leave on a plate until dry. Serve in small paper cases.

Recipes for reference

In the following chapter you will find a number of simplified basic recipes for pastry, stuffings and dumplings, as well as quite a few of the most popular sauces, both savoury and sweet. I think you will discover they are not only time-saving, but will also do much to add that special 'finishing touch' to the meals you serve.

French dressing

you will need:

6 tablespoons corn oil	pinch dry mustard
2 tablespoons vinegar	¼ teaspoon salt
pinch pepper	1 level teaspoon sugar

1 Put all the ingredients into a small screw-top jar and shake well.

With onion, parsley or tomato: A little finely chopped raw onion or chopped parsley, or 2 teaspoons tomato purée, may be added to the above dressing, if liked. Adjust seasoning to taste.

Never-fail mayonnaise

you will need:

¾ teaspoon sugar	pinch pepper
½ teaspoon dry mustard	1 egg white
	6 tablespoons corn oil
½ teaspoon salt	3 teaspoons vinegar

1 Mix sugar, mustard, salt and pepper in a basin. Blend in the egg white and beat well.
2 Continue beating, adding the corn oil a little at a time, until half is used.
3 Add 2 teaspoons vinegar, then the remaining corn oil, beating all the time.
4 Beat in the remaining 1 teaspoon vinegar.
5 The mayonnaise can be stored if necessary, in a covered jar in the refrigerator. This quantity makes about ¼ pint.

Quick salad dressing

no cooking

you will need:

2 teaspoons French mustard	5-oz. carton plain yoghourt
1 tablespoon granulated sugar	seasoning

1 Blend the French mustard with granulated sugar.
2 Stir into the yoghourt. Add salt and pepper to taste.

With onion: A little finely chopped raw onion or chives may also be added.

Hollandaise sauce

cooking time: 1–2 minutes to reduce vinegar

you will need:

2 tablespoons white wine vinegar	3 oz. unsalted butter lemon juice
2 egg yolks	salt and pepper

1 Put the vinegar in a small pan and boil until the quantity is reduced to 1 tablespoon.
2 Leave to cool, then mix with the egg yolks in a basin.
3 Place the basin over a pan of hot water and whisk until the eggs begin to thicken.
4 Gradually whisk in the butter, adding a little at a time.
5 Add lemon juice and season carefully.

Cream salad dressing

you will need:

¼ teaspoon made mustard	1 tablespoon oil
¼ teaspoon salt pepper	1 dessertspoon vinegar (a mixture of malt and tarragon)
pinch castor sugar	
2 tablespoons thick cream	

1 Mix the mustard, salt, pepper to taste and castor sugar together. Stir in the cream.
2 Add the oil drop by drop, stirring all the time.
3 Add the vinegar slowly and stir well.

White sauce

cooking time: about 10 minutes

you will need:

1 oz. butter	½ pint milk
1 oz. flour	seasoning

1 Melt the butter, stir in the flour using a wooden spoon.
2 Cook over a gentle heat for 3 minutes without browning, stirring throughout.
3 Remove from heat and gradually stir in half the milk, stir hard until well blended.
4 Return to heat, cook slowly until sauce thickens, stirring.
5 Gradually add remaining liquid.
6 Bring to boil, season with salt and pepper. Allow to boil for 2–3 minutes, stirring throughout.
7 This is a thick or coating sauce, used for cauliflower cheese, filling flans and baked casserole dishes.

For a thin or pouring sauce, use ½ oz. butter and ½ oz. flour. The amount of milk and method are the same.

Cheese sauce: To ½ pint white sauce add 2 heaped tablespoons grated cheese, a little mustard, a little salt and a pinch of cayenne pepper. Add the cheese when the sauce is at boiling point, mix in well but do not allow the sauce to boil.

Mushroom sauce: Cook 2 oz. sliced mushrooms in ½ oz. butter very gently for about 15 minutes. Stir the mushrooms, butter and the juice from the mushrooms into ½ pint hot white sauce. Season.

Onion sauce: To ½ pint white sauce (made from ½ milk and ½ liquid in which the onions were cooked) add 2 chopped, boiled onions and a few drops of lemon juice.

Egg sauce: Stir 1 or 2 chopped hard-boiled eggs into white sauce, after it has boiled.

Sweet sauce: Omit seasoning, stir 1 oz. sugar and 2 or 3 drops flavouring essence into ½ pint hot white sauce. Stir until sugar is dissolved.

Tomato sauce

cooking time: about 30 minutes

you will need:

2 onions	pinch thyme
2 tablespoons oil	1 pint water
1 small can tomato paste	salt and pepper

1 Peel and chop the onions.
2 Heat the oil in a small pan and fry onions for about 5 minutes.
3 Add the tomato paste and cook for a few minutes longer, stirring all the time.
4 Add the thyme and water, boil gently for about 25 minutes. Season to taste.

Curry sauce

cooking time: 20 minutes

you will need:

2 tablespoons corn oil	½ teaspoon salt
1 medium-sized onion, sliced	2 level tablespoons tomato purée
1 level tablespoon curry powder	1 beef stock cube
3 level teaspoons cornflour	1 pint water
	2 tablespoons chutney

1 Heat the corn oil and sauté the onion until tender.

2 Stir in curry powder and cornflour and cook for 1 minute.
3 Stir in salt, tomato purée, beef stock cube, water and chutney.
4 Bring to the boil, stirring all the time. Simmer gently for 15 minutes.

Sweet sauce

cooking time: about 10 minutes

you will need:

1 level teaspoon cornflour	2 tablespoons jam or marmalade
½ pint water	few drops lemon juice (optional)

1 Blend the cornflour with a little of the water.
2 Bring the remainder of the water, together with the jam, to the boil. Pour on to the cornflour, stirring all the time.
3 Rinse the pan with cold water, pour the sauce back and bring to the boil. Boil for 3 minutes, add lemon juice to taste, if liked.

Apple sauce

cooking time: 20–30 minutes

you will need:

1 lb. cooking apples	¼ pint water
½ oz. butter	1 strip lemon peel
2 oz. sugar	(optional)

1 Peel and slice apples.
2 Put all ingredients in a pan and cook until the apples are reduced to a pulp.
3 Remove lemon peel, if used, and mash the apples well.

Lemon sauce

cooking time: about 10 minutes

you will need:

4 tablespoons sugar	1 oz. butter
1 tablespoon cornflour	grated rind and juice
pinch salt	1 lemon
½ pint water	pinch grated nutmeg

1 Blend sugar and cornflour and salt to a paste with a little of the cold water.
2 Bring the remaining water to the boil, pour on to blended cornflour, stirring throughout.
3 Pour into pan, bring slowly back to boil, boil about 3 minutes stirring constantly.
4 Beat in butter, add lemon rind and juice and grated nutmeg.

With ice cream: This sauce is delicious served piping hot over chocolate or vanilla ice cream.

Quick orange sauce

cooking time: 5 minutes

you will need:

1 packet white sauce	½ lemon
½ pint milk	1 dessertspoon red
1 orange	wine

1 Make up white sauce according to the directions on the package but use only ½ pint milk.
2 Add juice of 1 orange and ½ lemon and 1 dessertspoon red wine.
3 Add finely shredded peel of ½ orange.
4 Correct seasoning as required and serve with duck and pork.

Syrup sauce

cooking time: 5 minutes

you will need:

2 tablespoons treacle or syrup	1 dessertspoon lemon juice
¼ pint water	

1 Boil the syrup, water and lemon juice for 5 minutes.
2 Strain and serve.

Caramel sauce

cooking time: 8–10 minutes

you will need:

4 rounded tablespoons soft brown sugar	2 oz. luxury margarine
4 level tablespoons golden syrup	4 tablespoons water

1 Place the sugar and syrup in a pan. Heat and stir until dissolved.
2 Bring to the boil and simmer for 2 minutes. Allow to cool.
3 Add margarine and water.
4 Return to the heat and boil for 2 minutes.
5 Allow to cool again and then serve with ice cream.

Coffee sauce

cooking time: 2–3 minutes

you will need:

½ pint strong black coffee	2 heaped tablespoons sugar
3 level tablespoons arrowroot	1 oz. luxury margarine

1 Blend coffee and arrowroot together.
2 Place in a small saucepan, bring to the boil and simmer gently for 2–3 minutes.
3 Remove from the heat, cool slightly, and stir in the sugar and margarine.

Jam sauce

cooking time: 5 minutes

you will need:

¼ pint water	1 tablespoon jam
1 oz. sugar	few drops lemon juice

1 Boil water and sugar for 3–4 minutes.
2 Stir in jam and lemon juice.
3 Bring to boiling point and strain.

Note:
If red jam is used add a few drops of cochineal to improve the colour.

Marmalade sauce: Make as jam sauce, substituting 1 tablespoon marmalade for jam.

Cornflour sauce

cooking time: about 5–10 minutes

you will need:

1 teaspoon cornflour	1 dessertspoon castor sugar
½ pint milk	
strip lemon rind	

1 Mix the cornflour with a little of the milk.
2 Heat the remainder of the milk with the lemon rind.
3 Pour the hot milk on to the cornflour, stirring continuously with a wooden spoon.
4 Boil for 5 minutes stirring all the time.
5 Remove the lemon rind and add the sugar.

Egg custard

cooking time: about 15 minutes

you will need:

½ pint milk, short measure	1 dessertspoon sugar
2 egg yolks	few drops vanilla essence

1 Add a little cold milk to the egg yolks and heat the remainder of the milk.
2 Pour the hot milk over the lightly beaten yolks and milk, stirring well.
3 Return to the rinsed pan, and cook, stirring constantly until the mixture coats the back of the spoon.

4 Add sugar and vanilla essence to taste.
5 Serve hot or cold.

To make a custard tart: This custard may be used to make a custard tart. Pour into an un-cooked pastry case, see page 87, and bake in a very moderate oven (350°F – Gas Mark 3) until the custard is set.

Icings

Water or glacé icing

you will need:

8 oz. icing sugar   approx. 1½ dessertspoons warm water

1 To cover the top of a 6-in. sponge use 4 oz. icing sugar; for a 7 in. cake or sponge use 6 oz. and for an 8–9 in. sponge use 8 oz.
2 If covering top and sides use at least double quantities.
3 If the icing sugar seems rather lumpy you can sieve it, but if you add the water and let it stand for some time, unless the lumps are very hard indeed, it will become smooth by itself.
4 Add the water gradually.

Chocolate glacé icing: Add 1 good dessertspoon cocoa to the icing and then beat in a knob of butter melted.

Coffee glacé icing: Mix with strong coffee instead of water or with soluble coffee powder, blended with little warm water.

Lemon glacé icing: Mix with lemon juice instead of water.

Orange glacé icing: Mix with orange juice instead of water.

Vanilla glacé icing: Add a few drops of vanilla essence.

Milky bar icing: Melt 1 large Milky bar and 2 tablespoons water together in a bowl over hot water.
For coating – add 4 oz. sieved icing sugar.
For spreading – add 6 oz. sieved icing sugar.
For piping – add 7 oz. sieved icing sugar.
For rolling out – add 9 oz. sieved icing sugar.

Colour with vegetable colouring to suit the cake.

Mocha glacé icing: Add 1 good dessertspoon cocoa to the icing sugar and use strong coffee instead of water. A small knob of melted butter can be added if liked.

Spiced glacé icing: Blend ½ teaspoon mixed spice, ½ teaspoon grated nutmeg and ½ teaspoon cinnamon with the icing sugar.

Almond glacé icing: Add a few drops almond essence.

Butter cream

you will need:

6–8 oz. icing sugar   vanilla essence
4 oz. butter

1 Sieve the icing sugar.
2 Beat butter with a wooden spoon or spatula until soft.
3 Beat icing sugar into the butter, adding a few drops of vanilla essence. The amount of icing sugar needed will depend on the consistency of the cream required.

Orange or lemon butter cream: Add finely grated lemon or orange rind and juice, to taste, to the creamed butter and sugar. Beat hard to prevent curdling.

Walnut butter cream: Add 2 tablespoons finely chopped walnuts to creamed butter and sugar and mix thoroughly.

Almond butter cream: Add 2 tablespoons finely chopped toasted almonds to creamed butter and sugar.

Coffee butter cream: Make as basic butter cream. Omit the vanilla essence and use 2 teaspoons coffee essence.

Mocha butter cream: Make a coffee butter cream, adding 2 oz. melted chocolate, as well as the coffee essence.

Chocolate butter cream: Make as coffee butter cream, adding 2 oz. butter until soft. Blend in the melted chocolate and 3 oz. sieved icing sugar.

Basic easy-mix pastry method

Ingredients	7-in. crust	8 in. crust	7-in. single crust or 9-in. single crust
Corn oil	4 tablespoons	4½ tablespoons	5 tablespoons
Iced water	1½ tablespoons	2 tablespoons	2½ tablespoons
Plain flour	5 oz.	6 oz.	8 oz.
Salt	pinch	pinch	¼ level teaspoon

1 Pour measured corn oil into mixing bowl, add required amount of iced water, whisk with a fork until an emulsion is formed.
2 Sift flour and salt together. Gradually stir into the corn oil and water mixture in the bowl.
3 Continue stirring until a workable dough is formed. Slightly more or less flour than stated may be required according to measure used.
4 Place pastry between two sheets of greaseproof paper. Roll out to the required size.
5 Remove the top sheet of paper. Ease the pastry into the pie plate, then peel off the remaining sheet of paper. Press the pastry well into the dish and neaten the edge.

Short crust pastry

you will need:

8 oz. flour
pinch salt
2 oz. margarine

2 oz. lard (or vegetable shortening)
cold water to mix

1 Sieve the flour and salt into a mixing bowl.
2 Roughly chop the fat and add to the flour. Rub the fat into the flour using the finger tips until the mixture resembles breadcrumbs.
3 Gradually add the cold water and knead mixture lightly by hand until it works together into a firm dough.
4 Turn out on to a lightly floured surface and knead lightly until smooth. Turn pastry over and roll out, as required.
5 For baking times see individual recipes using short crust pastry.

Rich short crust pastry

you will need:

8 oz. flour
pinch salt
5 oz. butter
1 egg yolk

1 teaspoon castor sugar
1–2 tablespoons cold water

1 Sieve flour and salt into a bowl.
2 Rub the butter lightly into the flour, using finger tips, until the mixture resembles breadcrumbs.
3 Add sugar and egg yolk, work into the flour, adding water gradually until the mixture forms a firm dough.
4 Turn on to a floured surface, knead lightly and roll out. If a pastry is difficult to handle, leave in a cold place for at least half an hour before using.
5 For baking times see individual recipes using rich short crust pastry.

Flaky pastry

you will need:

8 oz. flour
pinch salt
6 oz. fat – use butter or equal quantities of margarine and lard

squeeze lemon juice
cold water to mix

1 Sieve flour and salt into a bowl.
2 Cream the fat until soft and pliable, and divide into four portions.
3 Rub one portion of the fat into the flour, add a squeeze of lemon juice and sufficient cold water to make a soft dough.
4 Roll the dough into an oblong. Cover ⅔ of this with another portion of the fat, dabbing the fat in small pieces over the dough.
5 Fold the dough in three, starting at the bottom with the uncovered section. Bring this up to the centre of the oblong. Bring the top third down over this. Lightly press the edges together with a rolling pin.
6 Half turn the pastry to the left and roll it out into an oblong.
7 Repeat this process (Nos. 5 and 6) twice, adding another portion of the fat each time.

8 Fold the pastry in three once more, without adding fat.

Wrap the pastry in greaseproof paper or foil, and leave in the 'fridge or a cold place for an hour before rolling out for use.

If possible leave the pastry to 'relax' in a cool place for about 10 minutes between each rolling.

Rough puff pastry

you will need:

8 oz. flour
pinch salt
6 oz. butter – or equal
   quantities of
   margarine and lard

1 teaspoon lemon juice
cold water to mix

1 Sieve flour and salt into a bowl.
2 Cut the fat into small cubes, add to the flour. Do not rub in.
3 Add lemon juice and sufficient cold water to mix to a fairly stiff dough.
4 Roll out into an oblong, taking care not to stretch the pastry at the edges.
5 Fold the pastry into three. Bring the bottom end two thirds across, and bring the top piece down to the folded edge.
6 Seal the edges by pressing lightly with a rolling pin.
7 Half turn the pastry to the left and roll it out into an oblong.
8 Repeat this process (Nos. 5 and 6) twice.
9 Fold the pastry in three once more, wrap it in greaseproof paper or foil and leave it in a 'fridge or cold place for an hour before rolling out for use.

This pastry is very similar to puff pastry but is easier and quicker to make. It can be used in any recipe which requires puff or flaky pastry.

To make a flan case

1 Make pastry (see page 86 and above).
2 Roll out pastry into a circle about 2 inches larger than the flan ring.
3 Place flan ring on a baking sheet. Place the round of pastry over the ring and press into shape, taking care that the pastry fits well against the inside edge but that it is not stretched.
4 Trim off surplus pastry by passing the rolling pin over the edge of the tin. Place a piece of lightly greased greaseproof, greased side down,
in the flan and fill with uncooked rice, haricot beans or macaroni.
5 Bake in a moderately hot oven (375°F – Gas Mark 5) for 15 minutes or until the pastry is firm. Pastry baked in this way is described as 'baked blind'. This is done to ensure a good shape. The rice, etc., can be stored in a jar and used indefinitely for this purpose.
6 Remove filling and paper from flan. Return flan to oven for a further 5 minutes to allow base to cook through.
7 Remove flan ring and leave flan case on a wire tray until cold. Cold cooked pastry may be stored in an air-tight tin and used as required.
8 If a flan ring is not available a sandwich tin may be used but, before the pastry is fitted, strips of strong paper should be placed across the inside of the tin to protrude at the edges. This will enable the flan case to be removed easily from the tin after cooking.

Suet pastry

you will need:

8 oz. flour (with plain
   flour, use 1 teaspoon
   baking powder)

pinch salt
4 oz. shredded suet
water to mix

1 Sieve flour and salt and baking powder, if used.
2 Add suet and mix in, using a long-bladed knife.
3 Stir in enough water to make a firm dough.
4 Knead lightly, roll out as required.
5 For cooking times see individual recipes using suet pastry.

Savoury dumplings

cooking time: 15–20 minutes

you will need:

4 oz. flour (with plain
   flour use ¾ tea-
   spoon baking
   powder)

2 oz. shredded suet
good pinch salt and
   pepper
water to mix

1 Mix all the ingredients together, adding enough water to make a firm dough.
2 Lightly flour the hands and roll the dough into 8–12 small balls.
3 Add the dumplings to the stew, soup, etc.,

when it is at simmering point – about 15–20 minutes before the end of the cooking time. Make sure the stew does not go off the boil while the dumplings are cooking.

Bacon dumplings: Make as for savoury dumplings, adding 2 rashers of lightly fried bacon, cut into small pieces, 2 tablespoons chopped parsley and 1 tablespoon tomato ketchup. Serve with boiled rabbit or bacon.

Cornish dumplings: Make as for savoury dumplings, but cook in boiling salted water. Drain well and serve with boiled meat.

Mixed herb dumplings: Make as for savoury dumplings, adding 1 teaspoon dried mixed herbs or 2 teaspoons freshly chopped mixed herbs.

Parsley dumplings: Make as for savoury dumplings, adding 1 tablespoon finely chopped parsley. Make the dough into smaller balls and cook for 10 minutes only. Serve with boiled chicken, rabbit or ham.

Sausage meat dumplings: Make as for savoury dumplings, adding 4 oz. pork sausage meat and ½ teaspoon dried sage.

Kidney dumplings: Skin and core 2 sheep's kidneys, cutting each into 4. Divide savoury dumpling dough into 8 balls and tuck 1 piece of kidney into each ball.

Sage and onion stuffing

cooking time: 10 minutes

you will need:

4 large onions	1 oz. butter or
10 fresh sage leaves	margarine
or 1 teaspoon dried	1 level teaspoon salt
sage	½ level teaspoon
4 oz. fresh	mustard
breadcrumbs	

1 Peel the onions and boil them for 5 minutes.
2 If fresh sage leaves are used, dip them in boiling water for a minute.
3 Chop or mince the onion and sage leaves.
4 Melt fat and thoroughly mix all ingredients.

Veal forcemeat or stuffing

you will need:

1–2 oz. suet	1 level teaspoon dried
1 tablespoon chopped	thyme or savoury
parsley	pinch mace
½ level teaspoon	½ level teaspoon salt
grated lemon rind	¼ level teaspoon
2 oz. fresh	pepper
breadcrumbs	1 beaten egg and milk
	to mix

1 Use only 1 oz. suet if stuffing fatty meat.
2 Grate the suet.
3 Wash, dry and chop parsley.
4 Finely grate lemon rind.
5 Mix ingredients together, binding with beaten egg and some milk if necessary.

Index